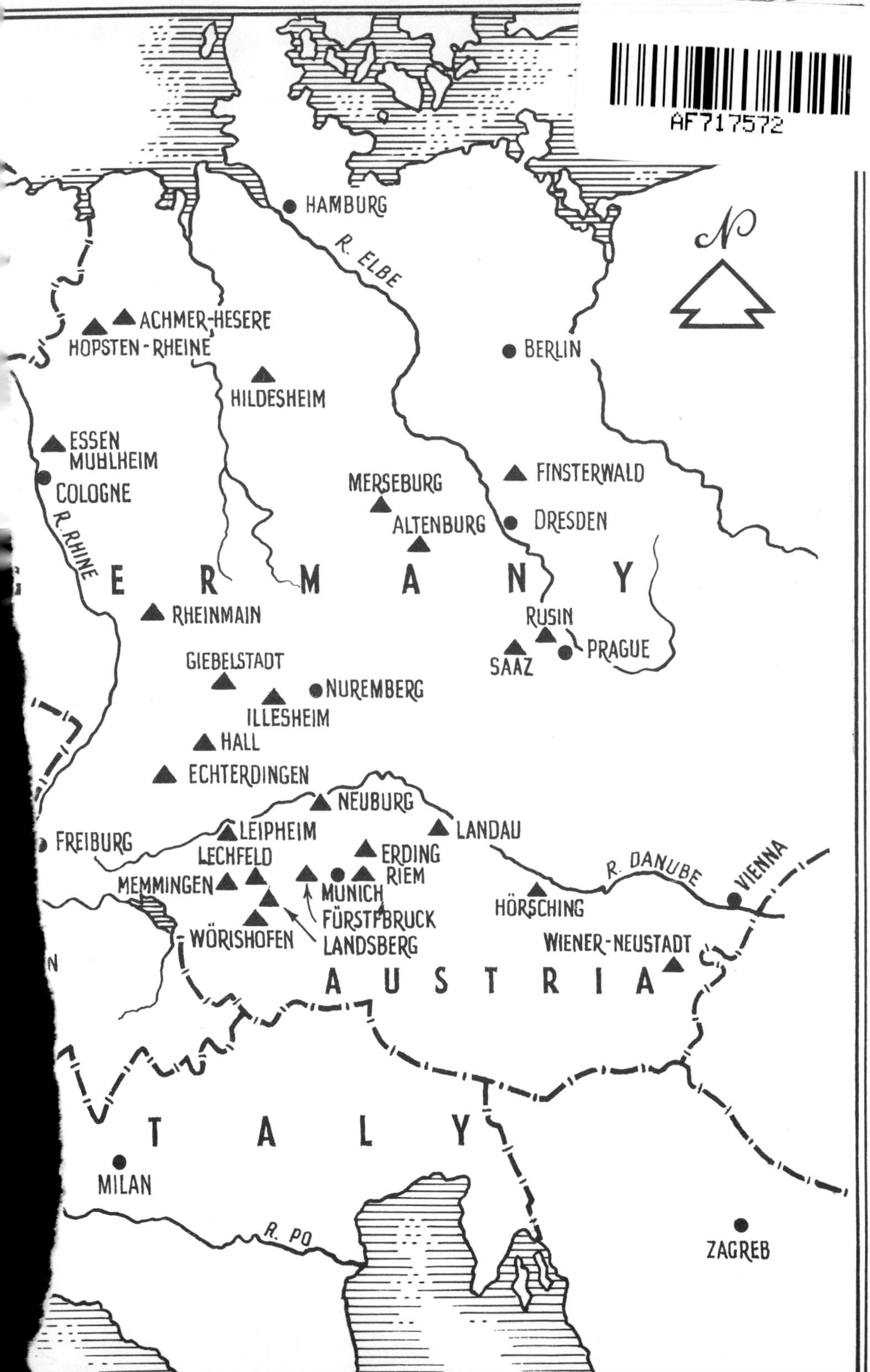
HAMBURG
R. ELBE
ACHMER-HESERE
HOPSTEN-RHEINE
BERLIN
HILDESHEIM
ESSEN
MUHLHEIM
COLOGNE
MERSEBURG
FINSTERWALD
ALTENBURG
DRESDEN
R. RHINE
GERMANY
RHEINMAIN
RUSIN
SAAZ
PRAGUE
GIEBELSTADT
NUREMBERG
ILLESHEIM
HALL
ECHTERDINGEN
NEUBURG
LANDAU
LEIPHEIM
FREIBURG
LECHFELD
ERDING
RIEM
R. DANUBE
VIENNA
MEMMINGEN
MUNICH
FÜRSTFBRUCK
HÖRSCHING
WÖRISHOFEN
LANDSBERG
WIENER-NEUSTADT
AUSTRIA
TALY
MILAN
R. PO
ZAGREB

# *Kampfgeschwader 'Edelweiss'*

WOLFGANG DIERICH

# *Kampfgeschwader 'Edelweiss'*

The History of a German Bomber Unit, 1935–1945

LONDON

**IAN ALLAN LTD**

First published 1973
English Edition 1975

ISBN 0 7110 0601 6



Translated by Richard Simpkins

Edited by Alfred Price



Published by Ian Allan Ltd, Shepperton, Surrey.

Photoset, printed and bound
in Great Britain by
REDWOOD BURN LIMITED
Trowbridge & Esher.

# *Contents*

# *Foreword to the English Edition*

by ALFRED PRICE

For many of us who lived in wartime Britain, the most distinct first-hand memories of the *Luftwaffe* bomber force were the wambling note of its aircraft flying overhead at night, the whistle of the bombs it dropped, and sometimes the heartening sight of one of its aircraft which had been shot down. It was at all times a remote force whose members were, seemingly, lacking in feeling or even form. Now, for the first time in the English language, we have in Wolfgang Dierich's book a story which gives us a vivid insight into life in a German bomber unit: *Kampfgeschwader 51*, the Edelweiss *Geschwader*.

Of the units in the German bomber force *KG 51* had what was probably the most interesting history. Although the *Geschwader* did not take part in the Polish campaign it was involved in almost all the major actions after it: in France and the Low Countries, the Battle of Britain, the night *Blitz* on Britain, the Balkans campaign, Russia, the 1944 night attacks on Britain and finally, with the revolutionary new Messerschmitt 262 jet fighter-bomber, in the last desperate actions in the west. For a short time, *KG 51* even operated in the bomber-destroyer role against the American daylight raiders penetrating into Germany.

Reading Dierich's account the first thing that struck me was its similarity in places to some of the accounts I have read of RAF bomber operations; indeed, apart from the different (but similarly untried) aircraft and the different targets, the stories of the early high-level German leaflet raids almost duplicate those of the RAF. The sky itself has plenty of hazards for friend and foe alike.

In this book we learn what it was like to be on the receiving end of RAF Fighter Command's attentions: there was the remarkable act of airborne chivalry by Spitfires over Dunkirk; the terrible battering suffered during one action in the Battle of Britain, when *KG 51* lost thirteen crews in one morning; the near-impotence of the British night defences in 1940 and 1941, and their formidable mettle in the spring of 1944.

Yet more important than the account of the operations over Britain, in gaining a general understanding of the Second World War, is that we are able to see how one German bomber unit fared in the terrible meat-grinder of a war in Russia. For us in Britain and America the great battles in the east were comfortably remote; it was not like that for the German army and air force. During the first three months of the Russian campaign, and in spite of the breathtaking German victories, the *Luftwaffe* sustained losses roughly equal to those it had suffered during the three months of the Battle of Britain. In Russia, however, instead of a clear end to the fighting at the end of the three months, the *Luftwaffe* found itself with an open-ended committment which was, in the years that followed, to bleed it white.

The essence of *Blitzkrieg* was that one risked heavy losses in order to secure a rapid and decisive victory; in Russia the Germans nearly succeeded, but nearly was not good enough. That does not mean, as some have suggested, that the concept of *Blitzkrieg* itself was at fault. Nor is there anything wrong in the principle of risking one's bombers in low level attacks on enemy positions, to support a rapid land advance. Even the purest believer in the value of air power would not quarrel with the thesis that, in a non-nuclear war against a strong and skillful opponent, the only certain way of knocking out his air force was (and is) to have one's army occupy the enemy homeland and with it his airfields. The fact that the Germans did not win in Russia, with their air force operating in the tactical role, certainly does not prove that they would have won by using it for strategic bombing (which is essentially a long-term weapon of attrition). In all probability the Germans would have done a lot worse, for without the *Luftwaffe* to support it on the battlefield their army would not have advanced as far as it did. The truth was that in attacking Russia before Britain was out of the way Hitler had bitten off somewhat more than he, or rather his forces, could chew. Once this particular die had been cast, the way in which the *Luftwaffe* was used was unlikely to effect the final outcome.

During the final year of the war *KG 51* operated the Me 262 jet fighter-bomber. A small detachment from the unit was declared operational and moved to France for action on July 20th, 1944—the day *before* No 616 Squadron of the RAF received its first two Gloster Meteors and began training. Thus *KG 51* was the first unit operational with aircraft powered by turbo-jet engines. During the months that followed *KG 51's* Me 262s provided many a British or American serviceman with his first glimpse into the jet age. To most of those who encountered them, the new German jets seemed virtually invulnerable as they darted across the sky, little disturbed either by the AA fire or the pursuing Allied fighters. In this book we learn the other side of the story: of the problems of pushing half-tested aircraft into action; of the under-developed and temperamental new engines with a running life of only about *eight* hours; and finally of the truism that even the fastest aircraft has to slow down to land, and when it does it is vulnerable to attack from aircraft of lower performance. Overshadowing the whole of the final chapter is the overwhelming Allied superiority on the ground and in the air, in the face of which the Germans were able to achieve little.

To sum up: Wolfgang Dierich's book contains much that will be new to English-speaking readers, and is an important addition to the works available to them on aerial warfare during the Second World War.

*March 1974* *Alfred Price*

# I *Early History and Buildup*

The *Luftwaffe* was officially unveiled on March 1st, 1935. Airmen from the First World War, and from the state airline *Lufthansa*, formed the nucleus of the force; they were soon joined by men from the army, the police, and from flying and gliding groups affiliated to the German League for Air Sport.

The embryo for *Kampfgeschwader 51* was the *Kampfregiment Merseburg* (first mentioned on October 1st, 1935), comprising the Merseburg and Finsterwalde *Geschwadern* equipped with the Junkers 52 bomber. At that time a *Geschwader* had the same status as an army battalion, and with an establishment of 39 aircraft corresponded in strength to a *Kampfgruppe* after the unveiling of the *Luftwaffe* in the spring of 1935. For security reasons the early *Geschwadern* were not numbered, and instead were referred to by the name of their base.

In the history of the *Luftwaffe*, 1936 was the year of the cadres. 'Mother' *Staffeln* were simply split into two, to form two 'daughter' *Staffeln*. To prevent *Staffel* commanders retaining their best men and using this system to rid themselves of 'duds', the local air district headquarters decided which Staffel would move out, and which one would remain.

On April 1st, 1936 *Kampfregiment Merseburg* was re-titled *Kampfgeschwader 153*. Its constituent units were now located as follows: Headquarters and *I Gruppe* at Merseburg, *II Gruppe* at Finsterwalde and *III Gruppe* at Altenburg. By the following June each of the *Gruppen* had received twenty-seven Ju 52s; they also operated a few Junkers W 34s, Ju 86s and Dornier 23s.

Once these aircraft arrived a start was made with specialist training in all fields. The individual *Gruppen* and *Staffeln* were quickly brought up to strength with young soldiers who had already completed the first months of their conscription. Until new ones were issued, the uniforms of every formation in the armed forces were to be seen around the stations.

Turich, the CO's observer, gives a detailed account of the training at Merseburg. Between December 13th, 1935 and February 4th, 1937 there was scarcely an airfield or airstrip in Germany that the 'Merseburgers' did not fly into with their Ju 52s, Do 23s and Ju W 34s. In between came circuits and bumps, navigation, cross-country and gunnery training flights. The charm of the locals—and even more the charms of the girls—made Stolp and Kolberg with the warm blue waters of the Baltic favourite weekend targets, though within the framework of air training and sporting activities.

There were many reasons why this comprehensive and exacting training took a high toll in casualties. From June to December 1935 the *Luftwaffe* had a monthly average of 48 crashes involving 12 deaths. Half these accidents were the result of breaches of flying discipline—a problem that will probably always be with us. Deviations from the laid-down flight plan, inadequate preparation and briefing, blind and bad-weather flying with insufficient training, irresponsible aerobatics (known to the initiated as 'mad-dog fights'), recklessness or negligence by the crew—in particular by the pilot—over the flying procedures for aircraft which were none too easy to handle at the best of times (The phrases 'flying coffin' and 'widowmaker' have their place in the airman's jargon of every era); these factors came up again and again in the findings of the Inspector for Air Safety and Equipment, Lt Col Ritter von Greim, who, as a result of this situation, took up his not very agreeable appointment on February 4th, 1936.

It was a crisis which posed a serious threat to the operational readiness of first-line units and logistic installations alike. And the rapid, precipitate buildup of five more bomber wing headquarters and eight squadrons during this year of 1935 did little to help the air safety situation.

At the end of 1936 the usual cries were voiced around that after cadre expansion parts of *KG 153* would soon be transferred to new stations in southern Germany. There was talk of fine cities like Nuernberg, Munich and Stuttgart. But no one believed it! They knew that new airfields were usually located very well away from the major centres of population and the diversions they offered.

In November 1936 one crew flew a Ju 52 from Merseburg to Lechfeld. From there they went on in an old jalopy through villages they had never heard of, and soon came to what was for those days an enormous building site. Construction trenches, large, half-finished accommodation blocks and hangars and a very long, wide firm stretch of grass, freshly laid, left little doubt that a new airfield was being built there. It was Memmingerberg, where planning and levelling had started in summer 1935 and where, as in many other places in Germany, work was pressed forward day and night—a veritable stamping of new airfields out of the ground. Before flying back the next day the crew had it drummed into them to keep their mouths shut—security was all important.

While the usual across-the-board training programme went ahead at Merseburg, Finsterwalde and Altenburg, intense activity continued at other military stations too. Air signals companies were formed for the new bomber *Geschwadern* to be stationed in South Germany; specialists from all arms were brought together to form the units which were to become airfield support companies, headquarters companies or station administrative companies. From industry came fully trained and highly-skilled technicians, to take their place in maintenance bays, on fitters' benches, in administrative posts and many other key branches. Finally in 1937 the security veil was lifted and the new stations were announced. The elements of *KG 153* were transferred to southern Germany.

Headquarters and *I Gruppe* from Merseburg were posted to Pensing near Landsberg. *II Gruppe* from Finsterwalde was to move to Leipheim, near Ulm/Guenzberg; and *III Gruppe* from Altenburg was transferred to Memmingerberg near Memmingen/Allgau. *III Gruppe* (Altenburg) had six months previously had to part with experienced crews to form the Condor Legion in Spain under the code-name 'Air Exercise Ruegen', and did not find the move exactly an aid to their training programme.

At Merseburg, Finsterwalde and Altenburg every available map was scanned in a feverish search for these strange places. Eventually the little villages were found on large-scale ordnance-survey sheets! Everyone said they were in the back of beyond; but they soon changed their minds.

In mid-February 1937 the advance parties were on the move at last, to get everything ready in the new stations where the station administrative companies had already done much good work. Messes, fitters' shops, workshops, administration and—most important of all—the canteens were already hard at it despite the work still going on on the buildings and installations. The official movement order was issued on March 1st, 1937. The formation's main bodies arrived at their destinations shortly after this, following a railway journey of many hours. On reaching their new stations, the airmen sometimes got a warm welcome from the locals, sometimes a rather hesitant one; but everyone quickly settled down and made his new surroundings a home-from-home among these warm-hearted, friendly Schwabians. Even though none of the stations were finished, at least the clean, well-designed accommodation, its local style blending agreably into the countryside, was very much to the taste of the airmen, who were eager to get on with their real work. The fields too were already usable for limited flying, at least in dry weather.

*III Gruppe* arrived at Memmingerberg on March 7th, 1937. A week later, when the *4th* and *5th Staffeln* and the headquarters arrived belatedly at Leipheim, things were looking a good deal better.

They had scarcely settled into the new station when training resumed, more intensively than ever. Certainly neither the aircrew nor the repair and servicing teams could complain of not having enough to do.

Instrument and radio navigation flights, formation flying, night and low flying, and long-distance flights to Tripoli and Rome (Afredo's for spaghetti), interwoven with regular gunnery and bombing practice with all types of aircraft in the *Geschwader* (Do 17, Ar 66, Do 23, Ju 52 and Ju W 34 and Fw 58) didn't leave anyone much peace. Things went so far that a book was run on who would be the first to loop a Ju 52, or who would be the first to put the notorious Do 23 into a dive and live to tell the tale.

The pride of the *Geschwader* was the then fastest bomber in the world, the Do 17 E (later 17 M), christened the 'flying pencil'. Everyone wanted to have a go on this aeroplane.

The first commander of the *Geschwader*, Lt Col Spang (an 'old eagle'), whose tour ran from March 1st 1937 to November 15th, 1938. Flying with his observer, Turich, in a 2-seater Arado 66, in two days he reconnoitred a total of 21 airfields in South Germany to ensure that, on mobilisation, he would have adequate diversion and dispersed take-off sites for his large force, now of almost 120 aircraft.

He took off from Landsberg at 04.55hrs on May 25th, 1937. Landing en route at Bad Aibling, Fuerstenfeldbruck, Memmingen, Leipheim, Giebelstadt, Wuerzburg, Schweinfurt, Kitzingen, Illesheim, Fuerth and Ansbach, he came in for the night at Ainring, only to take off again at 07.34hrs the following morning for Friedrichshofen, Freiburg, Karlsruhe, Herzogenaurach, Boeblingen, Ansbach, Neuburg, Schleissheim and Neubiburg. It was not until 18.49hrs that he touched down at Landsberg, the main station of his headquarters and his *Geschwader*.

Soon aircraft from the *Geschwader* were landing on all these fields, to get to know them and become thoroughly familiar with the surrounding country. Temporary ground facilities were set up and, in the usual flurry of wisecracks, everyone rushed off to reconnoitre the local 'facilities'.

Meanwhile the strength of the *Luftwaffe* had risen to a total of 11 bomber *Geschwader* headquarters, with 30 bomber *Gruppen* of 3 *Staffeln* each. With the annexation of Austria on March 12th, 1938, under *Plan Otto*, the *Geschwader* received its first mobilisation task and was called on to fly the 'paper round' (pamphlets on Vienna'), which was in those days a widely-practised form of aerial show of force to bring pressure to bear on the government and population of a country. This way of showing the flag is sometimes still used today.

On July 12th, 1938 the Air Force Inspector of Bombers (Air Force Inspectorate 2) took over the supervision of all bomber and dive-bomber units and responsibility for their well-being. Under him came the Bomber Schools, Air Gunnery Schools, the Anklam Navigation School, and the whole training of the Luftwaffe in navigation and bombing; the aim was to achieve a uniform standard of basic training among aircrew and groundstaff alike.

Once Austria had been incorporated into the German Reich, the crews of the *Geschwader* at last had the chance to admire the Alps between Innsbruck and Graz, which up till then had been no more than a glimmer on the southern horizon, and to add mountain flying to their experience.

Preparations for the large-scale autumn manoeuvres of 1938 soon made heavy demands on aircrew and technical personnel. The standard of flying discipline, skill and attainment that the *Geschwader* had achieved in its navigation and formation flying was disclosed over the National Socialist Party Convention at Dutzendteich near Nuernberg, when the *Staffeln* with their Do 17 Es flew past in mass formation at low level, to the delight of the spectators, German and critical foreigners alike.

The Supreme Commander of the *Luftwaffe* (Goering) congratulated the *Geschwader* on this, and awarded it squadron crests of Alpine flowers:

| | |
|---|---|
| I Squadron | Alpenrose (Alpine Rose) |
| II Squadron | Enzian (Gentian) |
| III Squadron | Edelweiss* |

Under the provisions of a planning study, the *Geschwader* received a code message on October 10th, 1938 and redeployed to airfields near the eastern border. On receiving another codeword *Sternflug* missions were flown over Czechoslovakia in the operations for annexation of the German-populated areas of the Sudetenland. Once again the 'weapons' were pamphlets and not bombs.

On May 1st, 1939 the *Geschwader* had to chip in its contribution to a further cadre expansion. *II Gruppe* at Leipheim was withdrawn from the *Geschwader* and transferred to Koeniggraetz to become *III Gruppe* and provide the nucleus for the *Kampfgeschwader 77* to be.

From May 15th to 25th, 1939 *I Gruppe* of *KG* 255 carried out a protracted exercise from the emergency strip at Bad Woerishofen. Used to strangers, this friendly spa made sure they did not suffer from lack of diversions. Everyone was delighted to escape from the military atmosphere of the barrack blocks and see civilisation once more.

To everyone's astonishment it was suddenly ordained on May 1st, 1939 that new *Geschwader* designations had been allotted en bloc. The machines had to be repainted.

Now the *Geschwardern* were: 1 (Hindenburg), 2, 3, 4 (General Wever), 26, 27 (Boelcke), 51, 53 (Condor Legion), 54, 55, 76 and 77. Lehrgeschwader 1 also counted as a bomber unit. Under these 13 *Geschwadern* headquarters, each with a headquarters *Staffel* permanently under command, came 30 bomber *Gruppen* with a total of 90 Staffeln.

* The Edelweiss (*Gnapthalium Leartopodium*) is sometimes known in English as 'lion's foot'.

These were:

| *Station* | *New Description** | *Name* | *Old Designation or Mother Unit* |
|---|---|---|---|
| Neubrandenburg Kolberg | I./KG 1 | Hindenburg | IV./152 |
| Sprottau/Liegnitz | I./KG 2 | Sledgehammer | II./252 |
| Liegnitz | II./KG 2 | | II.252 |
| Elbing/Heiligenbeil | II./KG 3 | Lightning | II./153 |
| Heiligenbeil | III./KG 3 | | III./153 |
| Gotha | I./KG 4 | General Wever | I./253 |
| Erfurt | II./KG 4 | | II./253 |
| Nordhausen | III./KG 4 | | III./253 |
| Luebeck-Blankensee | I./KG 26 | Lion | I./257 |
| Luenburg | II./KG 26 | | II./257 |
| Hannover-Langenhagen | I./KG 27 | Boelcke | I./157 |
| Wunstorf | II./KG 27 | | II./157 |
| Delmenhorst | III./KG 27 | | III./157 |
| Guetersloh | II./KG 28 | | II./254 |
| Landsberg | I./KG 51 | Alpine | I./153/255 |
| Memmingen | III./KG 51 | | III./153/255 |
| Ansbach | I./KG 53 | Condor Legion | I./355 |
| Schwaebisch Hall | II./KG 53 | | II./355 |
| Giebelstadt | III./KG 53 | | III./355 |
| Fritzlar | I./KG 54 | Death's Head | I./254 |
| Langendiebach | I./KG 55 | Gryphon | I./155 |
| Giessen | II./KG 55 | | II./155 |
| Wiener-Neustadt | I./KG 76 | | I./158 |
| Wels | III./KG 76 | | III./158 |
| Prag-Kbely | I./KG 77 | | I./153 |
| Bruenn | II./KG 77 | | II./158 |
| Koeniggraetz/Olmuetz | III./KG 77 | | II./255 |
| Schwerin | II./LG 1 | | II./LG 1 |
| Greifswald | III./LG 1 | | III./LG 1 |
| Neubrandenburg | I./LG 3 | | I./152 |

* I. /KG 1 = I Gruppe, Kampfgeschwader 1.

Above: Colonel Spang, left of centre, commander *Kampfgeschwader* 255 (centre, with Air Force sword) welcomes young aircrew to the new Station at Landsberg in 1937. Note the mixture of army and Nazi salutes.

Left: Colonel Alois Stoeckl, commander *III Gruppe KG 255*, Memmingerberg. He was killed in action over England on August 14th, 1940 when commanding *KG 55*

Bombers of the early years—a Do 23 of *KG 153* over Merseburg, 1937.

The Ju 86 provided an interim solution.

A Do 17 E of *KG 255* with a black circle in place of the Black Cross during the autumn manoeuvres, 1938.

In 1939/40 the He 111s were regularly spread to dispersal airfields like this one at Bad Woerishofen.

Captain Poetter, leader of 7th *Staffel*, *KG 51*, briefs his radio operator, Chief Warrant Officer Sepp Traut.

A He 111 of *7th Staffel* over the Bavarian Alps.

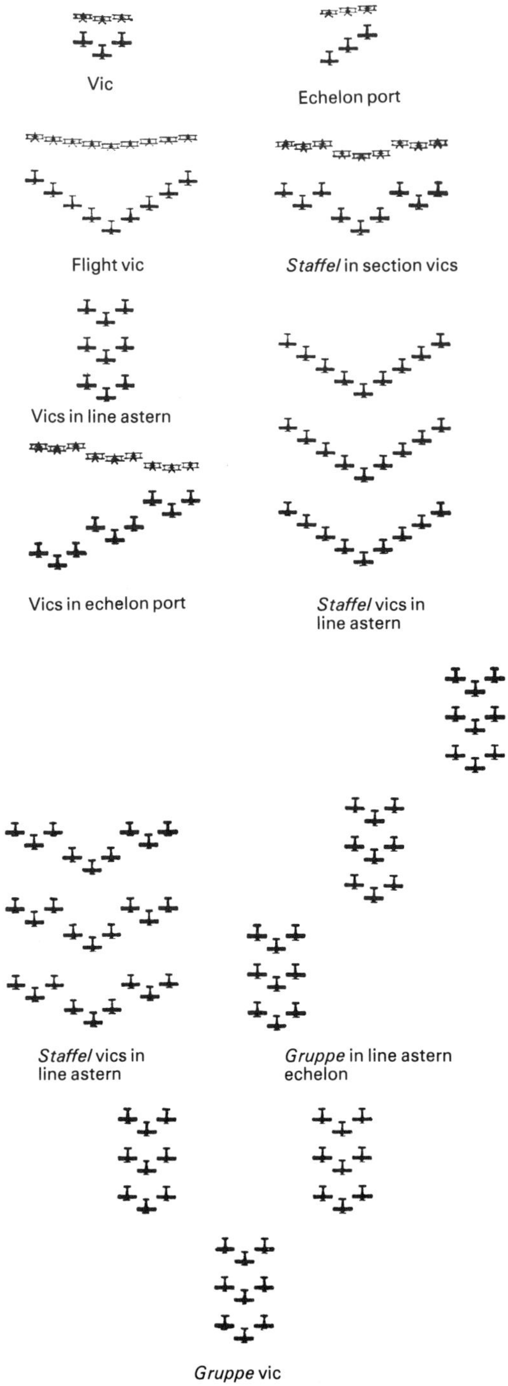


The most usual formations at the beginning of the war.

Ju88, 9K+HS of *III/KG 51* with markings appropriate to the Western Front, c. 1941.

Above: He 111 Hs of *KG 51* flying in over France, May 1940.

Above right: 1st Lieutenant Dr Stahl over Villaroche in his Ju 88 A1 fitted with home-made flame throwers, October 1940.

Right: Many specialists like Sergeant Zepf (right) could never get enough operational flying. These men were the hidden reserve for crews with gaps caused by illness.

Below: Field Marshal Hugo Sperrle in the airship hangar at Paris-Orly on November 12th, 1940. Major Marienfeld, commanding III Gruppe, *KG 51,* (left) reports his squadron present. On the right is Lieutenant Colonel Schulz-Heyn, commander *KG 51*.

Captain Kurt von Greiff (left) reports his *I Gruppe* present to Field Marshal Sperrle, with Captain Endres, Wing Adjutant.

A target photo taken shortly after the attack on the French airfield at Romorantin, 1940.

A Ju 88 A1 runs up its engines for a night take-off against targets in England, 1940.

Hits on Portsmouth Harbour, 1940.

French prisoners-of-war take part in clearance operations at Etampes-Mondésir.

Etampes-Mondésir, June 1940. Waiting to take off on a mission against England. Left-to-right: Major Kind, Chief Warrant Officers Lubrich and Goerres, 1st Lieut. Rath, Captain Brandt, 1st Lieut. Schwegler.

The *Geschwader* brings its dead to their last resting place in the Meaux cemetery. Major Marienfeld gives the graveside address. In the background, an Armoured Corps band.

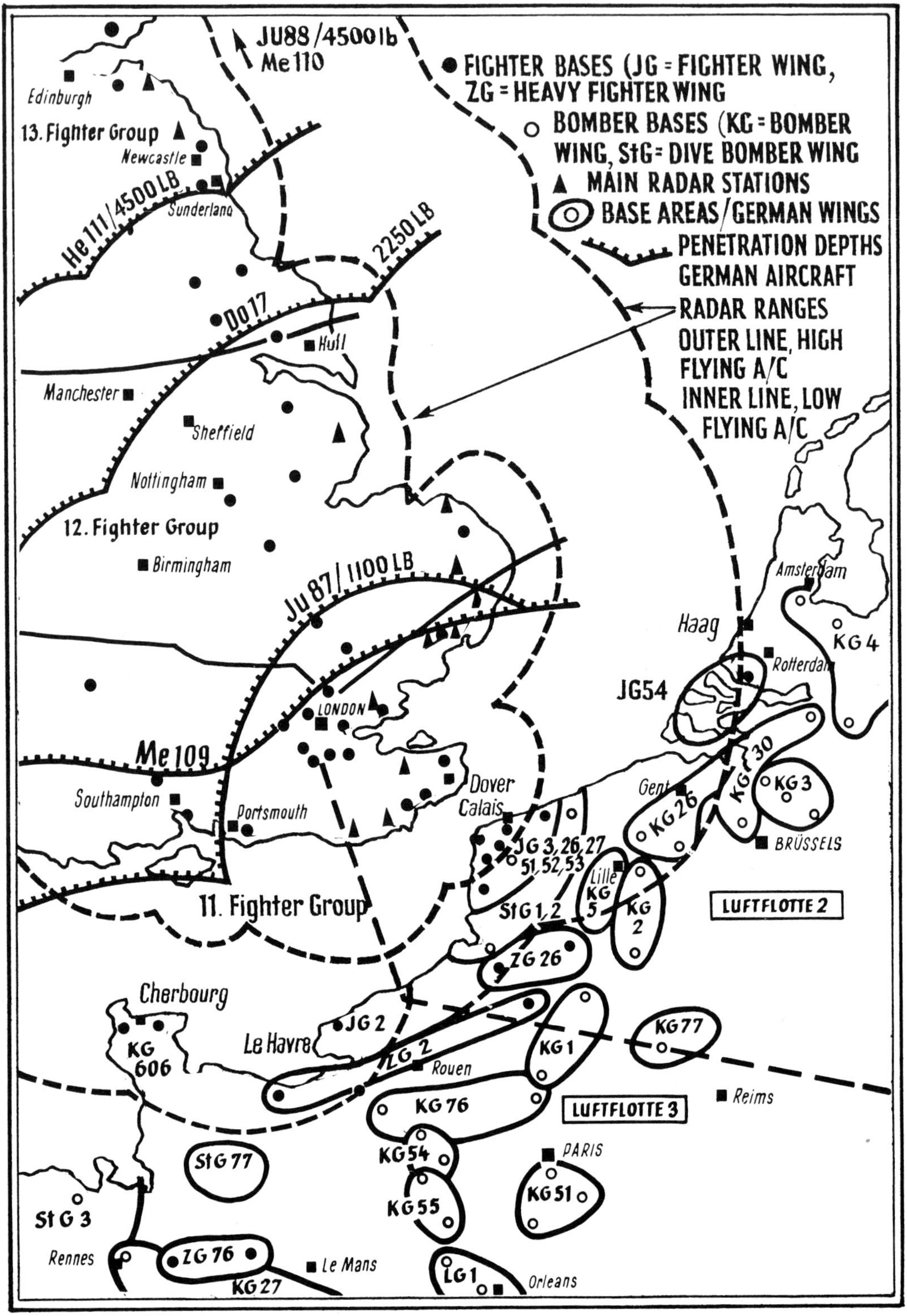


The deployment of operational formations during the Battle of Britain, 1940/41.

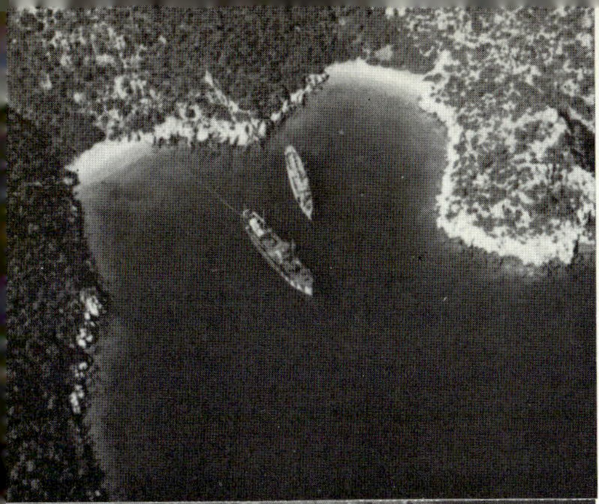

'Two into one does go', in the Gulf of Euboea, April 20th, 1941. The text of the report, prepared by *KG 51* Air Photo Section, reads: 'Northwest part of Gulf of Euboea—one 3,000–4,000 ton merchant ship sunk. Pilot: 1st Lieut. Schwegler, Observer: Warrant Officer Kraeher.'

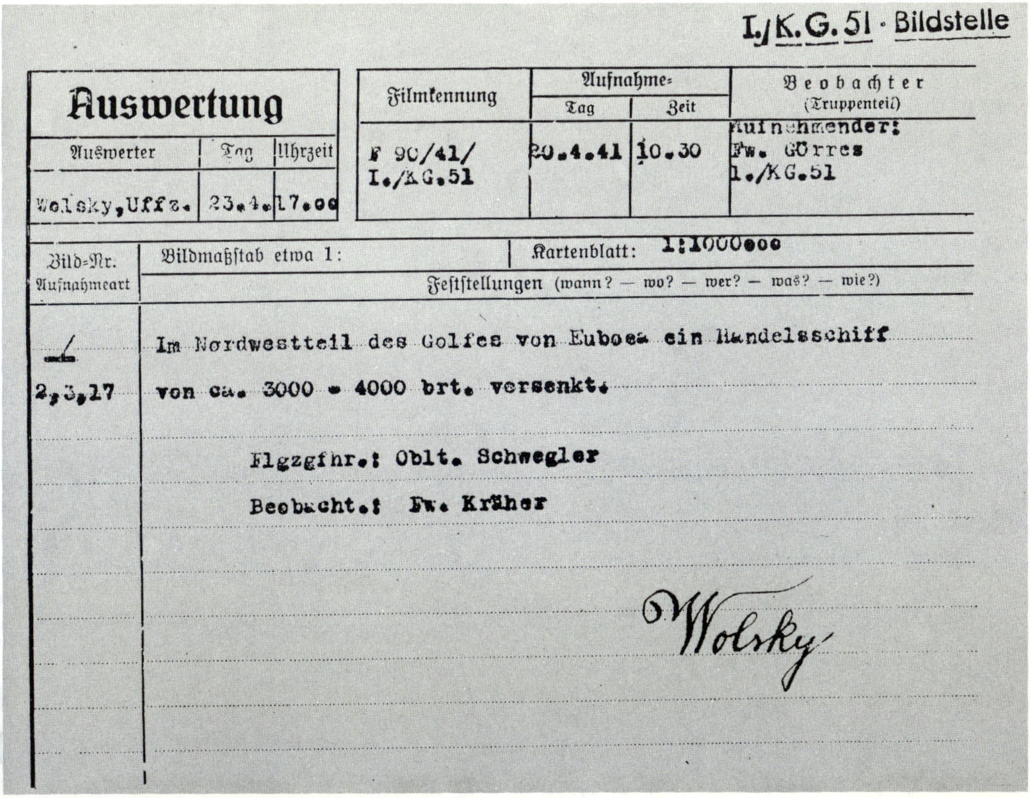

I./K.G. 51 · Bildstelle

**Auswertung**

| Auswerter | Tag | Uhrzeit | Filmkennung | Aufnahme- Tag | Aufnahme- Zeit | Beobachter (Truppenteil) |
|---|---|---|---|---|---|---|
| Wolsky, Uffz. | 23.4. | 17.00 | F 90/41/ I./K.G.51 | 20.4.41 | 10.30 | Aufnehmender: Fw. Görres I./K.G.51 |

Bild-Nr. Aufnahmeart | Bildmaßstab etwa 1: | Kartenblatt: 1:1000000

Feststellungen (wann? — wo? — wer? — was? — wie?)

2,3,17

Im Nordwestteil des Golfes von Euboea ein Handelsschiff von ca. 3000 - 4000 brt. versenkt.

Flgzgfhr.: Oblt. Schwegler

Beobacht.: Fw. Krüher

Wolsky

General Alexander Loehr gives a personal briefing on the operation against Yugoslavia. Left to right: General Loehr, Lieutenant Colonel Schulz-Heyn, commander *KG 51*, and Major Marienfeld, commanding *III Gruppe KG 51*.

Stick incendiary canisters falling on Belgrade, April 6th, 1941.

One of *KG 51's* most famous and successful crews. Left to right: 1st Lieut. Schwegler, Senior Warrant Officers Lubrich and Goerres.

Above: And where would Falimitse be? Somewhere in Poland, 1941; the forest of signs on the advance routes.

Left: The *Geschwader* Commander lands his Me 110 liaison aircraft in Krosno.

Lt Col. Koester, Commander of *KG 51* addresses his men on the occasion of the award, by Reichsmarschall Goering, of the first Trophy of Honour.

The transport section prepare their vehicles for a move.

A European rail tour for the technical personnel. Here they are moving from Paris to Wiener-Neustadt in March 1941.

Moves mean jabs. By regular inoculations, the MO, Dr Ott, otherwise known as Buddha, played his part in keeping the men fit.

Top: Bogged down again! Near the German hamlet of Strassburg during the advance into Bessarabia, 1941.

Centre: 'Well, who's going to kill it?' That was the question for Senior Warrant Officers Kratzert (left) and Lubrich at Balti in 1941. In the face of problems like this, the plague of mice was soon forgotten.

Right: Maria, the lovely gipsy, used to dance for her supper in Balti camp—but that's all she did. She lived with her tribe in some caves near the airfield.

Above: SD 2 fragmentation bombs were used against Russian routes and airfields at the opening of the Russian campaign in June 1941.

Below: Captain Hahn, commander of *I Gruppe KG 51* killed in action on February 3rd, 1942, and the grave of his crew near Tiraspol.

On August 1st, 1939 the calm before the storm was riven by another surprise. The Alpine *Geschwader* had suddenly to say goodbye to its beloved Do 17s and was ordered to convert, as rapidly as possible, to the He 111. This crash re-equipment within a fortnight (August 15th–30th, for both I *Gruppe* at Landsberg and III *Gruppe* at Memmingen) placed a very heavy strain on all members of the Wing, most of all on the aircrew and technical personnel.

On August 30th, 1939 *I Gruppe* with 36 crews was fully operational on He 111s. 'What's all the rush about?' everyone was asking. They got their answer with mobilisation for the Polish campaign; this as we now know, opened World War II. No-one ventured to think of the terrible consequences that this decision was later to bring in its wake.

On this fateful day the designation *Kampfgeschwader 255*, with its tactical sign '54+', was finally cancelled and changed to *Kampfgeschwader 51* (Edelweiss), tactical sign '9K+'. As war broke out the badge of III *Gruppe* at Memmingen became the crest of the whole *Geschwader*, a crest that it was to carry through the entire war, to almost every theatre; and a crest which gave it the name 'Edelweiss' *Geschwader* was to gain widespread fame.

Fate had determined, however, that KG 51 would receive its baptism of fire early—but not at the hands of the enemy.

September 27th, 1939 was a day of sultry heat at the remote Neuhasen emergency field, near Tuttlingen, close to the Swiss frontier to which 9 *Staffel, III Gruppe* and 3 Platoon of 7 Airfield Support Company had been dispersed. In the afternoon there was a bombing-up drill. Twenty 110lb bombs, which had been stacked on the edge of the field, were carefully driven in a truck over to aircraft 9K+LT. The team took great care in offloading them; they were not any too familiar with them yet. The tail of one bomb had a chalk-mark 'Fuze U/S', (unserviceable). In the next truck-load, as well as 20 bombs for 9K+FT, standing about 150 yards away, came a twenty-first which was carried across to 9K+LT by one man.

Corporal Kropp, the ammunition NCO, rushed up on his bicycle looking a bit excited and said: 'Where are the four bombs with U/S fuzes?' He wanted to stop the bombing-up. As these were not to be found round 9K+FT, they had to be beside 9K+LT. The truck followed him across. The bombs were found and lifted up on to the floor of the truck. The third bomb struck the floor hard and detonated with an ear-shattering explosion.

At that moment Senior Warrant Officer Schaale of 9 *Staffel* was checking the two automatic sequential bombing systems on 9K+LT, while Sergeant Held was oiling the bomb-doors. Both were killed. The Heinkel's port fuel tank was pierced by splinters, and as the aviation spirit ran out the machine burst into flames and was completely burnt out. Alarmed by the explosion and the black smoke cloud in the sky, men from all sections rushed to the scene of the accident and tried to salvage what was left, at great risk to their lives. Pilots and mechanics taxied nearby machines away to safety. The *Staffel* leader, Captain Brandt, called all who were helping back, as the fire was burning too fiercely to be put out and there was a risk of further explosions. Soon afterwards seventeen more bombs went off at short intervals, causing more appalling destruction.

In the ensuing enquiry, at Neuhausen, Memmingen, Baltringen and Landsberg were inspected. In some the fuze-retaining screw was missing, in others the springs of the fuze firing-pins were weak or corroded. Probably the fuzes of the bombs which caused the accident were cocked and not reset to safe, so that the bombs were fully armed and bound to go off at the slightest shock.

These first casualties of the war, on home ground, cost the unit dear. As well as Chief Warrant Officer Schaale of 9 *Staffel*, 3 sergeants, 2 corporals and 4 aircraftsmen of 7 Airfield Support Company and Corporal Kropp of Neuhausen Station Company were killed.

# *II The Campaign in the West*

The little copse round a grey watertower on the western edge of the Memmingerberg field in Southern Germany seemed to have been sited in the worst possible place by nature, quite apart from any air-safety requirement. No-one could envisage that this Memmingerberg landmark would make many a tired eye, returning from long-distance flights or operations, gladden at the sight of home. Many a time, especially at night, the hair of the controllers by the take-off flag would stand on end as the navigation lights of aircraft sweeping in to touch down would suddenly disappear into the dead ground that ran away outwards towards the city of Memmingen.

Now we had come from the splendid station at Altenburg, where the accommodation blocks blended so harmoniously into the gently rising slopes of the Leina Woods. So it was hardly surprising that we cast a rather jaundiced eye at the chaos of the Memmingerberg construction site. Barely two years later, one of the finest airfields in Germany had sprung into being. Between the blocks and the hangars trees and shrubs found good soil to grow on. And thanks to a go-ahead builder, the statutory static water tank happened quite by chance to have assumed the proportions of a large swimming pool.

The outbreak of war on September 1st, 1939 took many by surprise. Despite intensive training for war, most had probably hoped that the *Luftwaffe*—because of the power of its punch—would act as a kind of 'fleet-in-being' to keep the peace. Now the mobilisation plan had to be dragged out of the safe, and suddenly governed the start and progress of everything we did.

The first months of the war were for the *Geschwader* which did not take part in the Polish campaign, mainly a time of realistic redeployment exercises, bombing practice, camouflage and formation flying. The camouflage of our aircraft on the dispersal fields was often superb. One day, for example, the General Officer Commanding, Ritter von Greim, did not land at Neuhausen ob Eck as he had intended, because he thought his dispersal orders had not been carried out. He had not been able to spot the machines tucked away in the woods.

By dispersal to and camouflage on the previously reconnoitred emergency fields of Biberach, Bad Woerishafen, Reichenbach, Unterschlauersbach and Baltringen, it was hoped to forestall any French bombing attacks on the normal peacetime stations. In Landsberg for example beautiful darkling fir-trees were painted on the hangar doors to make them look like a wood. One evening some joker painted in one of these woods a larger-than-life, colourful Red Riding Hood complete with wolf. The delight of the astonished airmen was equalled only by the fury of district headquarters.

The operations which the *Geschwader* carried out during this first phase of the War were 'paper rounds'. Because of extreme weather conditions one such mission gave both valuable experience, and grounds for sadness. The 7th *Staffel* leader, Captain Poetter, reported it as follows.

*Propaganda operations by Kampfgeschwader 51 on November 17th, 1939*

To weaken the enemy's will to resist and to demonstrate the power and reach of German bombers, propaganda leaflets were dropped on France from time to time in the period between the Polish campaign and the offensive against France. During the Polish campaign *KG 51* had been the only bomber *Geschwader* to be held back in southwest Germany to cover possible action by our enemies in the West; it therefore played a major part in these operations.

In mid-November 1939 *III Gruppe* was located at the Bad Woerishofen dispersal field. We had received a quantity of propaganda material, packed together in stick form for fitting to the bomb racks. On release, a small barometric fuze broke the retaining bands of the packs. The leaflets, many thousands of them, were then scattered on the wind over wide areas of enemy territory. Among the leaflets was a series of large postcards, which made their point with the utmost delicacy. Below a white central panel was a dead French soldier hanging on a barbed wire entanglement; above it in large lettering: 'Où le Tommy est-il resté?' ('Where's Tommy got to?'). If you held the whole thing up to the light, you saw in vivid colours British soldiers disporting themselves with naked French women. Needless to say, this picture went down very well with our soldiers too!

On November 17th, 1939 the weather-men reckoned conditions were particularly favourable for a major long-range leaflet raid by day. Twelve He 111s from the *Geschwader* were used. Among the targets were Marseilles, Bordeaux, Nantes and Brest. From *7th Staffel* 1st Lieut Oechsle took off for Marseilles, and 1st Lieut Noelken and I for Bordeaux. We were to fly at 20,000 to 23,000 feet over solid cloud cover in a west to northwest wind of 38 knots. (Or that's what the forecast said.)

I was airborne at 08.25hrs. We climbed through the cloud to 23,000 feet and, after passing over the Black Forest radio beacon, set course direct for Bordeaux. Shortly afterwards the radio fixes started to look very suspicious to me. My observer, Lieut Stark was not very pleased about my not trusting his fixes. Finally all this fixing got so absurd that I assumed that we must somehow be getting one of those legendary land-bend effects from the Alps, and decided to fly on dead-reckoning alone.

After several hours the cloud-cover lifted and we tried to get a pin-point. But instead of seeing the sea ahead and to starboard, as we expected, we saw the Mediterranean, with the Gulf of Lyons to port. We fixed our exact position on the coastal lake of Sête. A very strong wind must have blown us right off course to port. In view of uncertainties of the wind conditions, fuel state and the fact that Marseilles was one of the planned targets, I decided to drop the leaflets northwest of Marseilles.

On the way back we took bearings on the Sottens transmitter in Switzerland, and these confirmed that unusually strong winds must be blowing from the northwest. With a fantastic wind correction angle—the nose of the machine was pointing somewhere towards Paris—we set course northwards to avoid crossing the Swiss frontier.

After a while I asked Lieut Stark for another fix but he did not reply. I looked over my shoulder and saw him sitting half-collapsed, with his face blue. He had severe anoxia, and if he didn't get oxygen soon he was going to die (in fact his oxygen lead had iced up). At that time we still had comparatively little experience of flying at great heights, but I knew that the only hope of saving his life was to go down quickly to around 10,000 feet. It was true that I didn't know whether or not we were over the Alps, but I felt that the very large course correction to the West should make us fairly safe.

So we dived steeply into the clouds. Sudden heavy icing on the propellers shook the aircraft, but at about 11,500 feet the 'patient' came to. I flew on for a time on the same course and, although I didn't think it would be much use, tried to get 'sensible' bearings from Switzerland and the Black Forest. Finally, as I was now also getting worried about the fuel state, I decided to get a visual on the ground at all costs—a decision which, in retrospect, everyone flying blind should be strongly dissuaded from making.

At 2,300 feet above sea level we caught our first glimpse of the ground through the ragged edges of heavy rainclouds. I went right down, flew along a railway line and managed to read on a station the name: Mirecourt. We found Mirecourt on the map, in France, 35 miles west of the Vosges. Heading East we flew up into the clouds, crossed the Vosges and the Black Forest, and finally landed at Woerishofen, after 6 hours and 50 minutes, under a cloudless sky. A little later 1st Lieut Noelken came in, after over 7 hours in the air and almost out of fuel. He was the only one to reach Bordeaux; despite doubts, he had trusted the fixes.

Debriefing on all sorties led to the conclusion that there must have been a northwest wind not of 38 knots but of 110 to 125 knots.

Of the twelve aircraft which had taken off, almost all had violated the Swiss and Italian frontiers. One machine landed in Italy and one in Slovakia. The Leader of the *8th Staffel*, Captain Plischke, crashed in the Alps on the Austrian–Italian border. His crew landed by parachute, some in Austria and some in Italy. 1st Lieut Oechsle ran into such turbulence over the Alps that his flight engineer suffered severe head injuries.

*The Luftwaffe* had absolutely no idea at the time that the mistral could produce such strong winds. As a result I was sent round to various bomber *Geschwadern* to lecture on my experiences in this flight.

From March 1940 the *Geschwader*, one of the most up-to-date in the *Luftwaffe* began conversion to the new Ju 88 bomber, with *I Gruppe* at Greifswald and *II Gruppe* at Barth. In some cases the pre-flight instruction lasted only a week. The robustness of the dive-bomber made it ideal for aerobatics. Everyone had a go at loops, rolls, Immelmann turns and stall turns, even if not with the full blessing of authority.

This rapid conversion to the sensitive 'race horse' took its toll. During dive-bombing training over Lechfeld, Warrant Officer Bier and Sergeants Stretz and Mueller crashed to their death at Bobingen.

On March 27th, 1940, Colonel Kammhuber arrived at his Headquarters, which had by then moved to Memmingen, to take over the *Geschwader*; he knew all about the serious problems of converting from the He 111 to the Ju 88. Apart from *KG 30* (Eagle), which was engaged primarily in maritime operations, there was still no 'land' bomber *Geschwader* equipped with this new dive-bomber. He just had to hope that the *Geschwader* would be given enough time to adjust properly to the new machine, before it was put to the test in operations.

This hope was not fulfilled. The first new aircraft arrived at the beginning of April, and the unit had to move to airfields with longer runways and night landing aids. *Geschwader* Headquarters moved to Lechfeld, and the newly re-formed *II Gruppe* to Fuerstenfeldbruck, near Munich. The elements to be employed on night operations went to Munich-Riem. The *1st* and *2nd Staffeln* of *I Gruppe*, and the entire *III Gruppe*, with crews experienced on the He 111 H, stayed for the time being at Landsberg and Memmingen and 3 did not complete conversion to the Ju 88 until the end of May.

Before the offensive began, crews of *KG 51* had already flown operational missions across the French frontier. Reconnaissance and 'paper-rounds' in the operational areas to be, such as Besançon, Luxeuil, Lure, Epinal and Bourges and even as deep as Bordeaux and Marseilles, had exercised the crews over strange ground under near-operational conditions. High level flights under cover of darkness and cloud were the order of the day.

The *Geschwader* was well-prepared for its forthcoming tasks in the West, notwithstanding the continuing conversion and re-equipment associated with the Ju 88, even though its serviceability (He 111 63%, Ju 88 53%) was below the *Luftwaffe* average. Having a total of 142 aircraft of two types (67 He 111s and 75 Ju 88s) spread over five different airfields (Landsberg, Bad Woerishofen, Lechfeld, Fuerstenfeldbruck and Munich), with only a small number of fully-trained men, was no easy situation to handle.

On the Friday before Whitsun, May 10th, 1940, with an H-hour of 05.35hrs, the German offensive in the West began. For *KG 51* the terse and pithy message was: *Execute Spessart Blue.*

1st Lieut Hermann Broeck, a young pilot in *9th Staffel*, wrote of it in 1942 in his book *'Bomber pilot over France'*: . . . then the staffel leader's telephone rang, and a moment later the order came: 'Rouse the staffel now; aircrew for briefing at 00.30hrs, warrant officer in charge of groundstaff to me immediately.' Seconds later the whole block sprang to life . . . Having given his short final briefing, the *staffel* leader, Captain Brandt, wished us luck and left the room.

I sat down at the table with my crew, went over once again every detail of the forthcoming raid and set about working out the navigation. 'It's OK, sir,' said my radio operator, Corporal Lerique, 'There's no need to worry about that. The boss'll show us where to do our stuff. He's got 130 missions under his belt already!' He was quite right; Brandt would lead us alright, for he had done a year's tour as a bomber pilot with the Condor Legion in Spain, where he had gained experience and shown his talents. Around us the other crews had also finished their preparations. As we were not to take off until 03.56hrs, there now began a lively discussion on what was going to happen in the next few hours and days. We talked about the strength of the French air defence and the odds of our hitting the target. Suddenly someone shouted: 'And we must reckon on our French colleagues leaving their calling cards with us. We're the nearest bomber unit to them. Then perhaps we'll be able to see for ourselves what our own *Flak* round the airfields can do.'

'I'd rather a fighter *Gruppe* met the French half way! I'd just love to have a ringside seat for a proper dogfight. For I reckon when we get mixed up with fighters ourselves it won't be much fun for us,' said another. None of us was in any doubt that we would soon be on the receiving end of a raid. A few years ago the French Air Force was the strongest on the Continent; surely they wouldn't just sit back and watch our efforts. These sort of thoughts made the time go quickly. At about

03.00hrs we wished each other luck, and went to our aircraft. At this moment there must have been thousands of German aircrew in the West walking over to their machines, ready to show the enemy what the *Luftwaffe* was made of. I thought of my parents, who were probably sound asleep and had no idea of all these great events. Everyone felt the greatness of the moment; we were seized by a feeling of pride and joy. At last we were off!

When we got to our 'Elector' aircraft the leading fitter reported it fit for operations, and wished us 'happy landings.' We helped each other into our parachute harnesses, and clambered aboard. I made a last quick check of the fuel state and armament. The bomb-aimer fussed over his sight and the radio operator tuned his sets. Then I started the engines; they both hummed away happily—a lot would depend on the way they behaved in the next hour or two, but we could trust them. All instruments were reading correctly. With a last wave to those staying behind we taxied to our take-off point. At that moment *7th Staffel* was taking off; well closed up, they got airborne. Then our *Staffel* leader's section began to roll, and it was our turn. My leader was Lieut Klischet, and I was flying as port wingman of this last section.

At a quick flash of his landing-light we revved the engines, and were away on our first operational sortie! This was in fact our first-ever formation flight by night, and I had my hands full keeping station on the lead aircraft. After a while the glass panels of our nose began to mist up, and I could see the leader's navigation lights only vaguely or not at all. The observer directed me; he could see out clearly from up top, and shouted changes of heading to me. On top of all this, the ground was completely hidden by a thick mist. Thus there was no sign of the French defences to be seen. After flying on westwards for a time without making anything out, I decided to turn back.

Fate had played us a dirty trick, and I was determined to take my precious bombload back home rather than drop it blind on French soil; which quite apart from being against orders, that could have been utterly stupid and purposeless.

Slowly the dawn broke . . . We could not be seen from the ground, but equally we could see nothing apart from a few steeples and the tops of isolated trees, which stuck up out of the mist. After a few minutes I got a fix on base, and so was able to head homeward.

At 06.34hrs we landed at base in a filthy temper. But I felt a bit better about things when I discovered that both the other aircraft in our three were already in, one an hour and one half an hour before us, and had brought their bombs back with them. Sorrow shared is sorrow halved! We thrashed out our unsuccessful sortie in great detail.

We felt pretty depressed as we watched our *Staffel* leader come in. The two wingmen landed first, and he touched down twenty minutes later. When we reported our failure to him, he consoled us in some measure, by telling us that we had acted quite rightly in the situation we were in. The first three had got through to the target and completed their mission.

Now we plagued our successful friends with questions over just how things had gone. The *Staffel* leader was caught by two French fighters on the way back, an attack which cost us our first casualties. His flight engineer had been hit twice in the head and was dead. The aircraft itself had taken a pasting; we counted 78 bullet-holes. But skilful evasive action and good shooting by the other gunners had prevented the fighters shooting the aircraft down. The other two aircraft in the section had come back unharmed without being intercepted by fighters. The *Flak* was pretty thick over the target—but to no effect.

As many as three sorties were flown that day by the young crews, some of them still green. Only an airman knows what it's like to hold his concentration for four hours flying at a time, pent up in a cramped crew-compartment. The crews had got up at midnight and it was eighteen hours before they came in from their last sortie and could snatch a restless sleep.

This first day of operations was overshadowed by a tragedy which touches the history of *KG 51* and of *III Gruppe* in particular. For bombs were dropped by mistake on Freiburg im Breisgau, a small German town in the Black Forest. So much rubbish, including some vicious personal attacks, was published about this after the War that it is proper to put the record straight.

For the 22nd mission against France on May 10th, 1940, *III/KG 51* was allotted Dijon-Longvic airfield as its primary target and the fighter field at Dôle–Taraux as its alternative target. Twenty He 111s took off from Bad Woerishofen and Landsberg between 14.30 and 14.41hrs with a full bombload and crews who were already tired from earlier sorties.

They flew in *Staffel* flight and assembled over the Landsberg Memmingen area at 5,000 feet above ground. It was very warm for the time of year, with stormclouds gathering over the Black Forest and the Vosges. They were ordered to cross the frontier at 20,000 feet and this forced the formation to fly through turbulent, dense cloudbanks in which one aircraft could barely see the next even though they were in close formation.

Dijon was bombed. Two French Morane fighters were confirmed shot down, with a third probable. One Section under the comparatively inexperienced Lieut Seidel lost the formation during the outward flight, owing to bad visibility over the Black Forest. The section flew on westwards, blind, and tried to find the target. The *III Gruppe* War Diary afterwards carried the report: 'This section made an independent attack on the airfield near Dôle from 17,000 feet. Three hangars and some accommodation blocks or workshops were identified. Hits were scored on hangars, accommodation blocks, the field itself and an AA position.'

Lieut Seidel, (who was later killed during the Battle of Britain) reported as follows:

'After taking off from Landsberg I had to fly blind at various times. Obviously I must have got off course. When our flight time indicated I must be near Dijon, I caught sight of the ground from time to time but could not fix my position. I then made various changes of course to get a pin-point through gaps in the cloud. Suddenly a major town loomed up ahead of me; I recognised it as Dijon and dropped my bombs on the airfield at H hour. Owing to bad visibility I could not observe the effect. After releasing my bombs, I set course for Landsberg, flying blind at times to begin with but then descending below cloud to keep the ground in sight.'

To this the *Gruppe* commander added:

'The interval between release time and landing time was so short that it could not possibly have been long enough for a direct flight from Dijon to Landsberg; but it matched the flight time from Freiburg to Landsberg well. It is true that a comparison of air photos of Dijon and Freiburg airfields shows a certain rough similarity, but Lieut Seidel admitted that the airfield he attacked could have been Freiburg. In any event he could not definitely state that it was not Freiburg. But the time of the return flight from release onwards was the main factor in leading Lieut Seidel and me to the horrifying conclusion that Lieut Seidel, after flying around and searching for some time, wrongly took the city of Freiburg, which suddenly appeared before his eyes, for Dijon. Lieut Seidel was deeply shaken when he learned this fact.'*

Twenty-two children, 13 women and 22 men were killed, and 20 children, 34 women and 47 men were injured as a result of the human—all too human—error of a qualified man and an unfortunate combination of circumstances. This tragic mistake by German aircraft was at the time, for reasons understandable enough as things were then, described as an *Allied* terror raid, and put to political use.

The first blow hit French Air Force installations, and was followed in

* Author's comment: The above statements were reconstructed after the war and clearly confuse Dôle–Tavaux with Dijon. The fields at Freiburg and Dôle–Tavaux are still (in 1970) in much the same shape as they were in 1940, apart from new building round them. Thus, the author, from his personal experience, cannot rule out the possibility that the two air bases had been confused. In similar weather conditions and with constant knowledge of his position, he found it difficult from 17,000 feet to get a positive first-time identification, although he *knew* the route he was flying.

the next few days by large-scale air support operations. *Luftflotte 3* covered the German armoured divisions of the 4, 12, 16 and 1 Armies of Army Group A, in their breathtaking advance through the Ardennes. *KG 51* worked mainly in northeast France, in front of the left flank of the German advance.

The first focal point of *KG 51*'s operations lay in the Sedan area, against lines of communication and troops in the French position on the Meuse. The normal routing was from Landsberg or Lechfeld via Mannheim and Trier, and then at very low level via Neufchâteau to Sedan. Lack of fuel usually took the aircraft in to Frankfurt-Rhein/Main or Giebelstadt, to fill up for the flight back to base.

In the large-scale raids of Operation Paula, against airfields in the Paris area, a technical defect forced Kammhuber to straggle from the formation during the return flight on June 3rd. Over Meaux on the Marne he provided a sitting target for French fighters, and was shot down. The crew survived the crash and was taken prisoner by the French —luckily not for long. Colonel Dr. Fisser took over command of the *Geschwader*.

Lieut Braeck has a tale to tell of an He 111 sortie on May 20th, 1940:

At 17.00hrs we took off again for the railway junction south of Compiègne. I was flying on the left of the leading vic in the *Gruppe*. This time we found a dense but thin layer of cloud at about 8,000 feet and flew on above it. Our fighter escort covered us. A few minutes before reaching our target, just after flying over the town of Soissons, the whole *Gruppe* went down through a gap in the clouds and flew on at 6,000–6,500 feet. After only a few seconds the French *Flak* began to get our range. Then two Moranes (French fighters) streaked out of the cloud and fired at me. They whistled past only about 30 feet below. 'What a cheek!' muttered my observer, as his machine-gun burst went short of them; he just didn't have time to aim. The radio operator reported that the French fighters had got into a dogfight with our own fighter escort, and had dived away. Their shots had hit our starboard wing, in a spot which was not at all dangerous. Meanwhile our duel with the AA gunners had started. I could see the tracer from my observer's gun racing earthwards like little sparks trying to overtake one another. Now we had our target, the railway junction, ahead. We could clearly make out how it bristled with medium AA guns. The muzzle-flashes were continuous; obviously this junction was very important for the French. I had never seen such a concentration of *Flak* round any target before.

We started our bombing run. As the observer was guiding me in, I happened to look down through the nose and noticed a tracer round coming straight at our nose. Instinctively I put the rudder hard over to port; everything happened so quickly. Two short sharp blows shook our machine. 'That was meant for us,' said Sepp drily, 'But where?' I couldn't see anything and had no time to look, because we were about to drop our bombs. There was another blow on my aircraft and at the same instant we heard a hideous rattle coming from outside—heavy *Flak* going off right beside us! The bombs were away and the formation swung off to port. An uneven whine in the engines suddenly made me prick my ears up. I got such a fright that for a fraction of a second the blood froze in my veins—engines damaged—forced landing—into the bag. These three notions suddenly added up in my mind to a dismal future. I had no time to look at my instruments but had to concentrate completely on the manoeuvres of the lead aircraft, to avoid ramming it. By playing with the throttles I tried to bring the engines to the same revs. No such luck! On and on went this horrible motor whine, coming and going—a noise to make a dead pilot turn in his grave. 'The bombs were spot on, sir,' Sepp called up from the underneath gun position—and in the same breath: 'We're losing all our oil, everything liquid is running out!'

We were flying straight again now, and I had a chance to check my engine instruments. It was true—the oil and coolant temperatures had already gone right off the clock. A glance at my starboard wing told me why—what a sight! I wondered why the wing was still there at all. Just to the right, near the motor, there was nothing left but a sieve about three feet long and eighteen inches wide. It must have been a direct hit, or at least a very near miss! The starboard engine was still running, although at reduced revs. But to avoid the risk of a fire I had to feather it, for the temperatures were still rising. I broke clear of the formation and radioed to the leader: 'Starboard engine out. Will try to reach base.' The *Gruppe* swept on past me. Four fighters stayed with me as escort, circling my plane, which was now flying at greatly reduced speed. In forty minutes I ought to be over our own lines. But what was that? Now the port engine began to run unevenly. That was all I needed! I throttled back and listened to the engine note. Now it was running smoothly again. But I should have to lose height because my speed was falling off. I had to battle for every hundred feet. I restarted the starboard engine, gave both engines full throttle and climbed with shuddering engines until the temperature gauge reached the stop again. Then I had to feather the starboard engine again, but we'd gained nearly 2,000 feet. And so it went on—up, and down again. Now we were over our own lines. With a farewell flip of the wings my fighter escort headed for home. I thought things over. I didn't want to make a forced landing in recently-occupied territory; with land communications the way they were, it would have taken us over a week to get back to our station. On we would go, then, till both engines finally seized up or we got to the first airfield on German soil. If the engine held out that long, I might even get back to base.

At 21.00 hrs and my friends had already landed when at last we saw the airfield below us. I had a good look at it from 3,000 feet, fired two red flares to indicate an emergency landing, and set about going in. With a certain amount of difficulty we managed to crank the undercarriage right down; but I didn't know whether it was damaged, and might collapse on touch-down. Anyway, we took care to strap ourselves in well. The field was not very large. All around it fighters were parked.

Then I got to the edge of the field but the speed was too high because the flaps wouldn't work—they had been shot away! We were half way across the field before I managed to get the wheels on the ground, and there we were, charging madly at over 80 knots towards a group of parked Me 109s with several fitters still working on them. 'That'll be some prang' the thought flashed through my mind. 'On to our belly for us, must get the undercart up' my brain was telling me. By now we were within about 400 feet of the other aircraft. Here we go! With a jerk I opened up the port engine and put starboard rudder on as hard as I could. Surely the undercarriage couldn't stand up to the violent change of direction and would break away! We swung sharply to starboard, about 60 degrees, and . . . rolled on in the new direction straight for a clear space at the edge of the field. There at least I wouldn't risk killing people or damaging aircraft. I steered through this gap and at last—at last!—having bounced over several ditches, came to rest in a potato field about 1,000 feet from the edge of the airfield. The undercarriage was still in one piece. That's the way it always is—if you don't want something to give, it's bound to break; if once in a while you try to smash something, it stands up to everything you do to it!

We climbed out, drew breath audibly and took a good look all round our 'Heinrich'. Meanwhile several crews from the fighter *Gruppe* which had escorted us and which happened to be stationed here, together with an engineer, came over and joined in our inspection of our dishevelled bird. There was no doubt about it—two hits with 40mm shell about 2ft 6in from the starboard engine, had shattered the main wing-spar and torn away about 22 square feet of the lower skin. These shells, bursting right near the engine, had punctured the whole of the nacelle and the oil and fuel tanks. As well as this there were several bullet-holes in the wing and hits from *Flak* splinters on the bottom of the fuselage. Before the end of the night I had reported our safe landing and the damage to the aircraft, to our headquarters. So we'd got away with it again! It was a miracle that none of us had been wounded, and this made all of us even more convinced that the bullet with our name on it had yet to be fired.'

On May 24th, 1940 Hitler issued the order for the German armour in front of Dunkirk to stand on the line Gravelines—St Omer—Béthune. Despite the battle-worn state of his units, Goering had arrogantly told the Fuehrer: 'My Fuehrer, leave the destruction of the enemy bottled up in Dunkirk to me and my *Luftwaffe*!' This meant a quick change of plan for *KG 51* too. Operations against French airfields and communications ended, and Dunkirk became the target.

The *Geschwader* flew one mission after another against the British troops who were pouring back towards Dunkirk from the Flanders front. The Allied Operation *Dynamo* for the rescue of the British Army had begun.

An incredible assembly of small ships and boats, fishing smacks, tugs with cargo lighters, private yachts and motor boats, all mixed up with destroyers and MTBs, and all stuffed full of soldiers, began to stream across the Channel. For the first time this operation was covered by 200 new Spitfires, which had been held in reserve; they inflicted heavy losses on the German bomber formations which attacked incessantly from early morning onwards.

*III/KG 51*, in its 53rd mission of the French campaign, put up twelve He 111s against troop concentrations round Dunkirk on May 27th, 1940. Major Kind, the squadron commander, took off from Landsberg on reconnaissance at 10.09hrs in his aircraft 9K + BD, followed by six machines from *7th Staffel*. The *8th Staffel*, with five aircraft under its leader Captain Schenk von Schweinberg, got airborne at 10.10hrs from Bad Woerishofen.

Heavy flak and numerous English fighters did not stop them from dropping 160 SD10 and 204 SC50 bombs on the target.

Lieut Gild's crew, LAC Kasseger, Sergeant Kannewurf, LAC Bartelt and Warrant Officer Goetlicher were reported missing and were later found to have been killed in action near Dunkirk.

About five hours later the Heinkels, some of them riddled with bullet and splinter holes, landed back at Frankfurt-Rhine/Main, where they were refuelled for the next operation of the day; holes were patched over and wounded crew-members received medical attention.

Two hours afterwards 8 He 111s from *7th* and *8th Staffeln* took off again and dropped 215 SC50s on their target, the port and town of Dunkirk.

1st Lieut Berger and his crew from *II/KG 51* were still a long way off when they spotted the giant pillars of smoke hanging in the sky. They had taken off from Lechfeld at 12.23hrs in their Ju 88. Tensely Berger and his observer, Senior Warrant Officer Blumhofer, concentrated on the ship that was their target. The start of the dive looked good. The ship began to take violent evasive action, and got outside the field of view of the bomb sight. They had to break off the attack. They pulled their fully-laden machine out and circled for the second dive. Sergeants Puls and Pertl were covering upwards with their MG15s. Just as Puls had changed an empty drum and started shooting again, he saw five lurking Spitfires just turning in for their first attack. After the first burst his machine-gun got a 'banana' (a burst barrel) and at the same moment the Junkers was crippled. One engine stopped, and Berger turned away for the safety of the coast. When the Spitfires saw that the crew with its crippled machine had stopped firing and could fire no more, they made a last circle, waved, and sat just off the wing-tips, escorting the lame duck for a while. Air warfare was still governed by a code of chivalry, albeit a harsh one.

Berger and his men wanted to bale out, but the hood jettison jammed, so they decided to make an emergency landing at Brussels. On flying over the field they fired red flares; the undercarriage wouldn't go down, Berger was bleeding from the shoulder and Puls was hit in the arm and eyes. With little hesitation Berger put the plane down on its belly. The crew spent several weeks in hospital near Brussels.

*I* and *II Gruppen* together flew 43 further Ju 88 sorties on that day. The inferno raged on. Dunkirk burnt and looked like a sea of flame. But it held out.

On May 28th and 29th, the weather was so bad that few bombs were dropped on the bridgehead; only in the afternoons could a few sorties be flown. And sea fog continued to hamper *Luftwaffe* operations up to May 31st.

On the morning of June 1st the weather cleared and the bombers resumed their relentless attacks. The devastating results made the British Admiral Ramsay confine movement of his evacuation fleet to the hours of darkness. Dunkirk fell on June 4th, 1940. 40,000 French soldiers were taken prisoner, having sacrificed themselves for the rescue of 215,587 men of the British Expeditionary Force and 123,095 French soldiers who were evacuated to England, later to form the cadres of new armies. The Supreme Commander of the German Air Force, Hermann Goering, had not kept his promise and had bled his forces white. The strength of *KG 51* in men and aircraft fell to less than half.

The unopposed occupation of Paris on June 14th was followed on June 22nd by the signing of the Franco–German armistice in the Forest of Compiègne, on the historic site where the Treaty of Versailles had been signed.

After the rapid advance, which in places had met with strong and damaging resistance, all units needed a pause for breath to regather their strength. But there was really little talk of rest. Everyone knew that the *Geschwader* was to move to airfields round Paris. Many a well-practised drill and elaborate plan had to be put into effect for establishing newly prepared bases on foreign soil. While all this was going on some crews still had to be converted from the He 111 to the Ju 88. Aircraft had to be overhauled in workshops, and everything had to be packed for the move.

The arrangements for the surface movement of groundstaff, who were already used to being stretched to the limit, gave little idea of the difficulties that would be caused by the damage to routes in France, then only newly occupied. The 7th Airfield Support Company, attached to the *Geschwader* had its fill in these days of getting to know roads and stations in Germany and France—a foretaste of what was to come later when they moved east. A company of this kind was necessary to make an emergency airfield into a functioning station. It was about 150 strong and was commanded by a reserve officer, usually one with technical training; he was backed up by the sergeant major, the pay officer, the quartermaster sergeant and chief cook, armoury and clothing sergeants and about 15 general duties men for office work.

Three technical platoons, each commanded by an experienced Senior Warrant Officer and 25 NCOs and men strong, serviced our machines by day and night. A workshop platoon of about 35 NCOs and men looked after the difficult major repairs, while the MT sergeant with his 22 drivers kept the company's extensive transport on the road. This included:

1 Mercedes staff car
5 Mercedes 6-wheeled trucks with trailers
4 Mercedes troop-carrying vehicles with extended bodies
3 other trucks
4 tractors
2 motor-cycle combinations

It is worth describing how this Airfield Support Company got moved around in the space of only six weeks. When the French campaign began it was transferred from Reichenbach (near Schussenried) to Landsberg to look after *III Gruppe*.

| | |
|---|---|
| May 23rd | Moved back to Reichenbach in support of a squadron of *KG 26* |
| May 27th | Back to Landsberg |
| June 2nd | Moved to Regensberg–Obertraubling for a quick briefing on the Ju 88. |
| June 9th | Arrived at Lechfeld |
| June 12th | Moved via Stuttgart and Mainz to Trier |
| June 14th | Moved on to Sedan |
| June 15th | At Villers Cottre |
| June 23rd | At Mondésir near Étampes (south of Paris) |

The airfield site at Étampes, like almost all the major French airfields, had been severely damaged by bombing and artillery fire. With the help of prisoners of war they set to to clear shattered hangars, level half the field and sort out accommodation so that the aircrew and machines could

Burning trains in Kupyansk station, 1941.

This is how 1st Lieut Unrau (aircraft 9K+BL) came back on October 12th, 1941. He was rammed by a Russian fighter over Eupatoria Bay. The starboard elevator was torn off and the rear of the fuselage twisted. The crew baled out over Bessarabia. 1st Lieut Feldmann took this remarkable photograph. See

Callsign 'Florian' with men of the air signals company in operations on the East Front.

The Tartars' Trench near Perekop, before the capture of the Crimea Peninsula, June 1942.

Sergeant Helmut Bernhard was one of the observers who, without pilot training, made a safe landing with a Ju 88 with his pilot dead on board.

Letters home had to be dashed off between missions. Here the armaments team do some hasty scribbling in Shitomir.

The hard winter of 1942 at Zaporoshye, where horse teams were used to tow aircraft . . .

. . . followed by a spring wallowing in mud at Nikolayev. But despite all the difficulties. . . .

. . . servicing was still done and sorties were flown. In the foreground are a Ju 88 engine and boxes of 100lb bombs.

Warrant Officer George Fanderl, the second member of *KG 51* to be awarded the Knight's Cross (on January 24th, 1942), welcomes 1st Lieut Loeffelbein at Tiraspol. On the right is Warrant Officer Graichen from Captain Hahn's crew, killed in action near Tiraspol on February 3rd, 1942.

Nikolayev, winter 1942. Snowdrifts made it very difficult to keep flying.

The Soviet cruiser *Krasny Krim*, sunk in Sevastopol harbour by the Fanderl crew.

Right: Captain Werner Baumbach, an experienced and well-known pilot in operations against shipping, flew several operations with *KG 51* in the Spring of 1942 against the Black Sea ports of Novorossisk, Tuapse and Suchoni. (See Appendix 'About These Bomber Pilots', p. 119.)

Above: Major Rath, commanding *III Gruppe KG 51* briefs crews for Operation Neptune (against Tuapse harbour). Left to right: Senior Warrant Officer Traut, 1st Lieut Sepp, Major Rath, 1st Lieut Kainz. (All were later killed in action.)

The railway bridge at Rostov-Bataysk in the spring floods of 1942.

Smoke cover over Tuapse harbour, 1942.

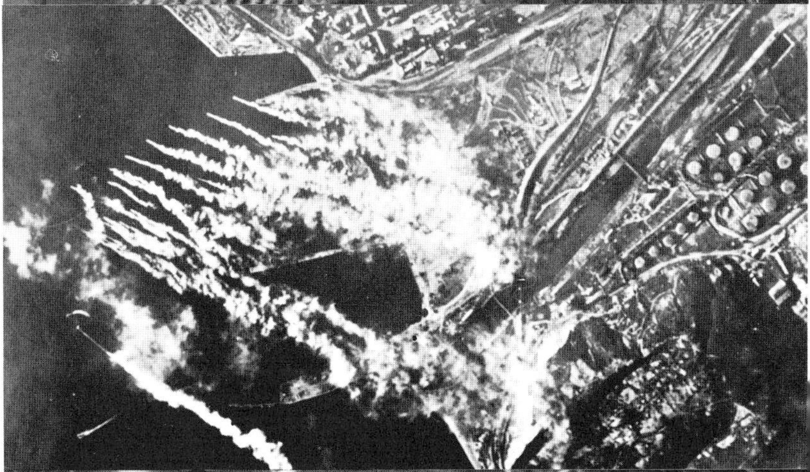

*III/KG 51*, attacks Tuapse harbour on March 23rd, 1942. At 15.10hrs, 9K+ED (Captain Haeberlen, Warrant Officer Boettcher, Sergeants Ernst and Gallermann) sank a Russian cruiser, hitting it with two SC500s and one SC250. The submarines, however, got off lightly.

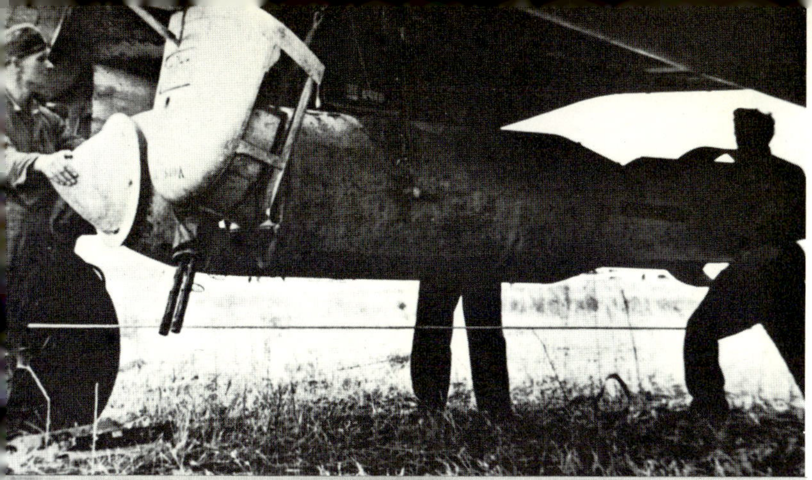

Bombing-up with the 1 ton blockbusters.

Kabardinka and the heavily defended bay of Novorossiysk, looking North, 1942.

A pasting from *Flak* over Novorossiysk, 1942.

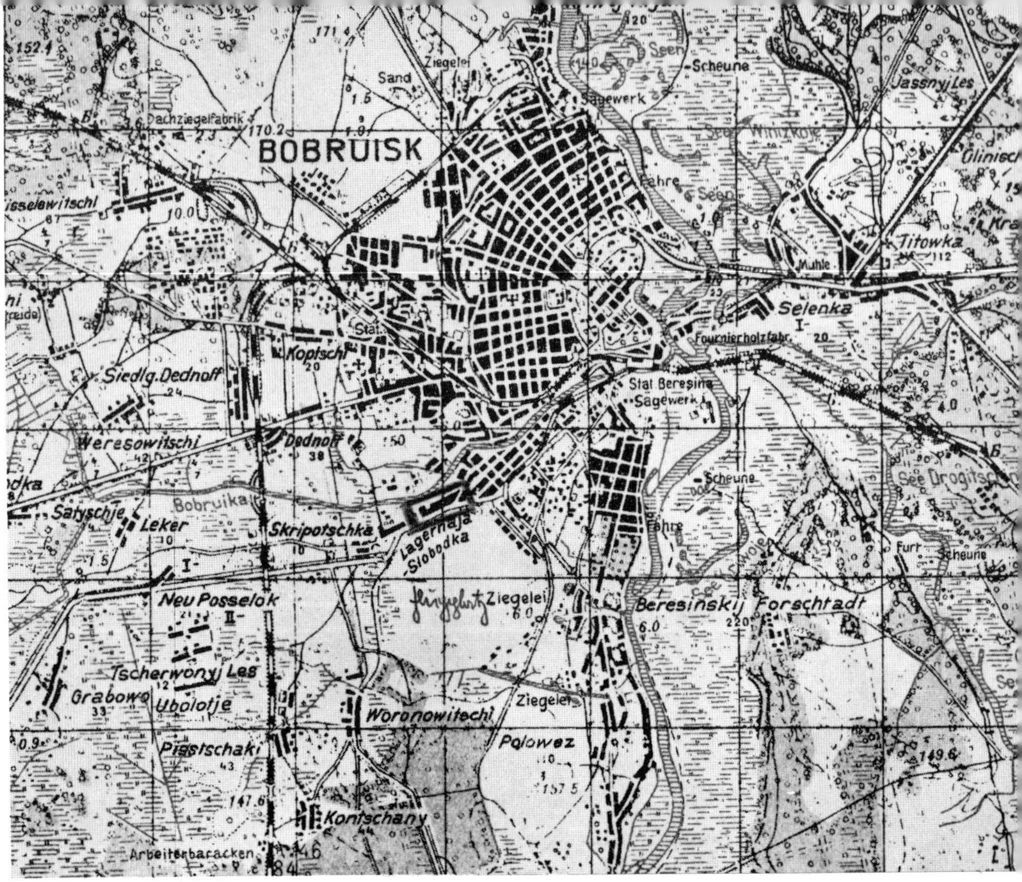


Map of Bobruysk on the Beresina, where most of the young crews were given their theatre orientation by *IV Gruppe*. (The airfield is indicated by a manuscript note lower centre.)

Crashed in flames. The end of an aspiring crew on the edge of the field at Seshchinskaya in 1943. From here the young crews used to fly their first operational missions for battle-inoculation. Their targets were the scattered partisan groups round Roslavl.

Only a few yards in it! A successful night belly-landing southeast of Taman.

Luck comes in all shapes. But in spite of a Chance light this landing at Tazinskaya was not without its problems.

Time I was home! Taxying in briskly at Wiener-Neustadt, this keen young pilot failed to spot a Me 110 that happened to be in the way. Fortunately it didn't belong to his own unit!

Ju 88 A4s of *KG 51* over the Crimea. In the background, the 'Table Mountain' near Simferopol.

Captain Matthias (Teddy) Schwegler, leader of *1 Staffel KG 51* at Sarabus. He was awarded the Knight's Cross on December 18th, 1942 and killed in action near Neuses/Ansbach on April 18th, 1945.

Above: A view over Sevastopol from the North. The deep bay of Severnaya is in the centre and Cape Khersonesskiy on the right. Clearly visible in the foreground are the fortified Sappun heights, heavily fought over in the battle of Sevastopol.

Below left: The *Flak*-raft in Severnaya bay, with its 164 guns, dominated the area by land, air and sea until 25th June 1942, when 1st Lieut Ernst Hinrichs hit and sank it. (Top—just before the attack; bottom—after the hits.)

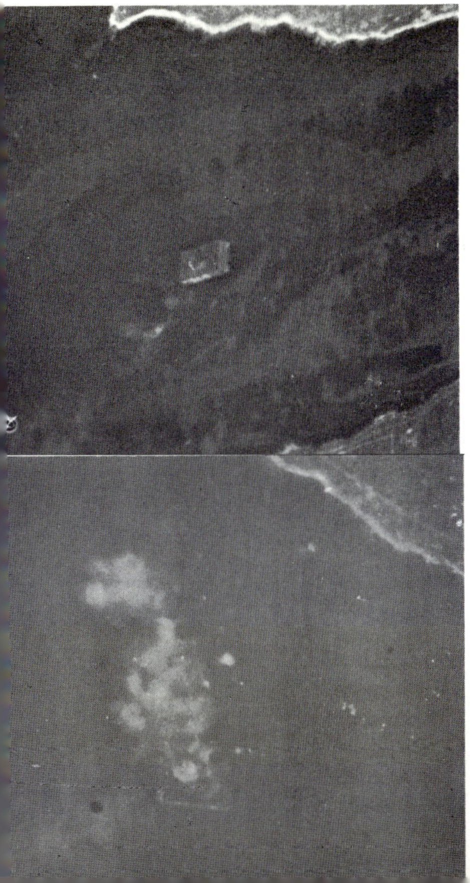

Above: 1st Lieut Ernst Hinrichs of *I/KG 51* was awarded the Knight's Cross on July 25th, 1942. He hit the *Flak* raft which had been causing so much trouble in his first dive. Exploding ammunition did the rest.

The remains of the fortress of Sevastopol.

An armoured train destroyed near Ossadovka.

Rostov airfield under attack. Later the *Geschwader* was stationed here in the difficult months of 1942/43.

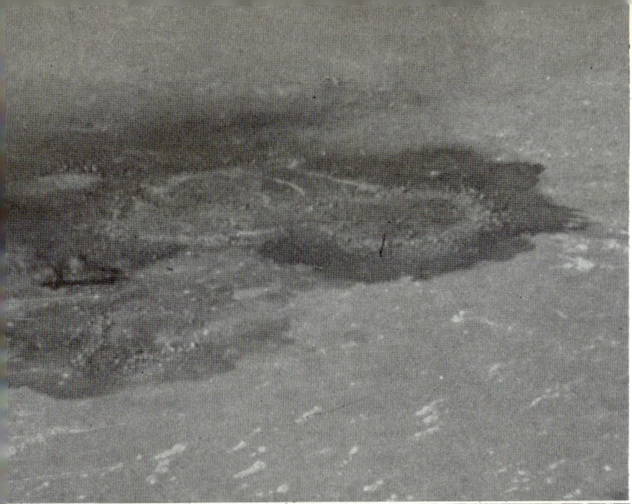

Above left/right: 1st Lieut 'Ali' Berger (above), leader of *1 Staffel*, set about bombing a Russian tank making its escape across the frozen Sea of Azov.

Although he hit only the ice, Ali marked up one tank sunk, surely a rare event in the history of air warfare.

Left/below: The Berger crew (from the left, Sergeant Sachs, Lieutenant Berger and Senior Warrant Officer Puls) scored a direct hit on a 4,000 ton Russian ammunition ship 4 miles north of Kerch. Detonations of shells of various calibres, caused by the exploding bombs, can be clearly seen.

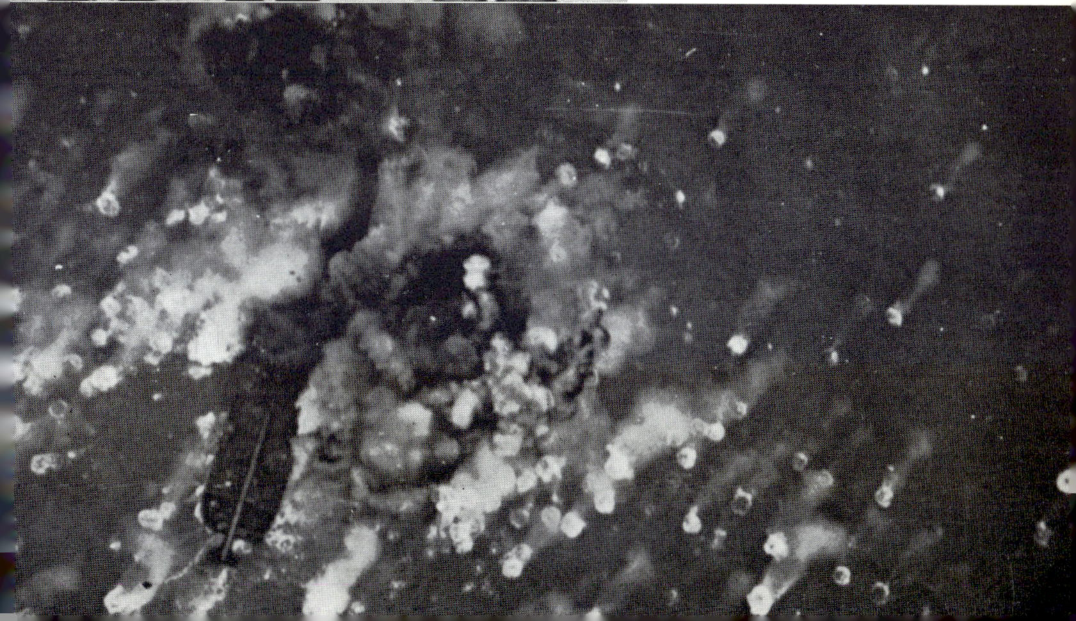

Despite direct hits from *Flak* on wing and tail, you have to be lucky sometimes.

The Schlegel crew are standing besides their aircraft. Left to right: Sergeants Stuhler and Haist, Lieutenant Schlegel, Sergeant Metz.

The arms of the city of Memmingen alongside the Edelweiss on the aircraft of Captain Haeberlen, commanding *I/KG 51*. Russia, winter 1942/43.

Here lies aircraft 9K+DB (Lieutenant Geruschke). Shot down by tanks near Alexandrovka on February 21st, 1943 he made a forced landing in no-man's-land. Lieutenant Winkel, showing great dash, landed nearby and rescued the crew from their predicament. (Both officers were killed in action later.)

The crew of callsign 'Wastel' standing beneath their Ju 88 A4. Left to right: Lieutenant Winkel, Sergeants Sieker, Ziemann and Schwachenwald, and the MO, Dr Denkhaus, who used to like flying with Winkel.

At the suggestion of Major Dierich, commanding *I/KG 51* a war cemetery for the dead of the *Geschwader* was established in the park of the Tartar castle of Bakhchisaray in the Crimea.

An attack on a station near Bataysk, 1943.

In Tatsinskaya they lived in do-it-yourself dug-outs. Next to flying, woodcutting was one of their most important daily tasks—to keep themselves warm.

at least be properly accepted. The first aircraft of *I/KG 51* flew in as early as June 18th to Paris-Orly, which had suffered relatively little damage. But because of lack of fuel not much flying could be done, and they had to switch to the well-built extended runway at Villacoublay. At the end of June the unit was able to occupy the quarters intended for it.

*Geschwader* Headquarters was with *II Gruppe* at the Château La Fontaine near Brétigny; *I Gruppe* first went to Château Villemain near Grisny-Suisnes and later joined *III Gruppe* in the castle barracks at Château Grand Yard near Voisenon. From there it was not far to the fields at Melun-Villaroche, which was quickly extended, Villacoublay, Brétigny and Étampes-Mondésir.

When the last crews to convert arrived at the end of July, they found their friends well set up. The history-packed area round Paris tempted them to long excursions to the palaces of Versailles and Fontainebleau or to more distant goals on the Loire, as far as Orléans.

The young dancers in the Place Pigalle and the topless night-spots of Montmartre provided diversion enough. The airman always likes his fun and his drink, and it was scarcely surprising that his purse should fall even wider open with the prospect of good French wine and the headiness of champagne. Commanders and *Staffel* leaders were not without their problems over what their men were getting up to.

On the occasion of an inspection by the Commander of *Luftflotte 3*, Field Marshal Hugo Sperrle, held in the giant, Zeppelin hangar at Paris-Orly in the presence of General Ritter von Greim, the first field promotions and awards for aircrew and groundstaff were read out. But this spell of comparative peace for rest and recreation did not last long. The next target was England, for the contest that was to go down in military history as the Battle of Britain.

## Review of Operations Against France

September 1st, 1939–June 19th, 1940
(*III/KG 51* only, no other records available)

59 operational missions with 434 sorties (all He 111),
of which 18 (32 sorties) were leaflet raids.

| | *Sorties* | *Flying Hours* |
|---|---|---|
| Reconnaissance *Schwarm* | 65 | 265 24′ |
| 7 *Staffel* | 148 | 614 18′ |
| 8 *Staffel* | 139 | 572 40′ |
| 9 *Staffel* | 82 | 321 59′ |

Bombs dropped:

| | |
|---|---|
| Total 373 tons | |
| SC10 | 956 |
| SC50 | 3,287 |
| SD50 | 3,779 |
| SC250 | 6 |
| Incendiary | 7,920 |
| SBe50 | 24 |

Ratio Incendiary : HE 1:1 approx.
Enemy fighters shot down: 14
Losses:
Killed 35
Wounded 20
Missing 4

# *III Operations Against England*

The ground organisation and final stations for the units of *Luftflotte 2* under Kesselring (Brussels) and *Luftflotte 3* under Sperrle (Paris) remained for a time in a bad state, with all the usual need for improvisation. Along the Loire, around Paris, past Brussels and as far east as Amsterdam the bomber *Geschwadern* lay poised, while the dive-bomber and fighter *Geschwadern* were focussed round Le Havre and Calais, nearer to the Channel because of their shorter range. *KG 51* was in *Fliegerkorps V* under Ritter von Greim, together with *KG 54* (Lt Col Hoelne, Evreux) and *KG 55* (Colonel Stoeckl, Chartres). The *Korps* operations centre was at Villacoublay.

Historical analyses differ over the phasing of events in the Battle of Britain; eight different versions are known to the author. From these he has chosen the account of the Swiss Dr Theo Weber, which in his view comes closest to the course of events as a whole.

The Contact Phase started at the beginning of July 1940 with armed photo-reconnaissance attacks on merchant shipping and harassing attacks on British port installations. These operations were conducted under orders at *Luftflotte* level, since no orders had yet emerged from the High Command. Bombing raids in force on the island Kingdom began on July 10th with the aim of drawing British Fighter Command to battle. *III Gruppe* flew only three sorties with its new Ju 88 A1s, these against targets in the Portsmouth area, which lay hidden under heavy cloud and rain squalls.

In occupied France the newly converted crews continued intensive training on their new aircraft. They familiarised themselves with the dive-bombing technique, flew bombing practices to improve accuracy, exercised in cooperation with the pathfinder unit *Kampfgruppe 100*, and gave the groundstaff a chance to work up the handling, arming, care and servicing of the Junkers. A few well-trained pilot-observers flew far and wide to find suitable diversion fields. Slowly they got used to the new area of operations. Up to the end of July they had taken part in only three major operations, the last one on July 29th being a mass night attack on armament and aero-engine plants and refineries in the Liverpool and

Southampton areas.

*Main Combat Phase I* began on August 8th, 1940, 'Eagle Day', after grand-tactical aims had at last been laid down in Air Force Command Directive No 17. The Royal Air Force was to be fought to a standstill as soon as possible, by the engagement of a wide variety of targets including armament works, the new and surprisingly effective radar stations, air bases and army camps. Terror raids were expressly forbidden.

At the start the weather impeded large-scale air operations. The majority of pilots in both our own and other *Geschwardern* were not yet sufficiently familiar with night operations, and there was no time or opportunity for training. For the attack of key targets, such as British aircraft and engine factories, special crews known as 'destruction crews' were designated. For this dangerous, often foolhardy task they received, over and above the usual flying duty pay, special danger money of 400 Reichsmarks—a lot of money at that time. These 'destruction crews' were drawn from crews outstanding in skill and achievement of each bomber wing. They were given full written briefs on their targets, but were not tied down to times or particular tactics or their unit operational procedures. They were directly responsible to *Fliegerkorps* for putting the targets out of action. The captain of a crew made his own assessment of weather and the air situation and finally decided for himself when and under what conditions he should strike. It would be superfluous to enlarge on the dangers of these operations; one needs only to consider that these crews flew their missions without fighter escort.

Lieut Dr Karl-Heinz Stahl and his crew, Schroeter, Noemeyer and Motes, carried out one of these special tasks on August 23rd, 1940. The target was the Test Centre at Farnborough. The account that follows has been written with the help of notes made by war correspondent Wolfgang Kuechler:

'The clouds hung low over our French operational air field at Villacoublay, so low that their fringes almost touched the ground. The crews sat around in a black mood. They had counted on having another little trip to England; and now it had been called off because of the weather. But they all stayed round the flight dispersal area. Mightn't there be something on after all? They were right. Only two minutes or so had gone by when the adjutant rushed out of the ops room waving a paper to say that one crew was to take off for a solo blind-flying raid. The target was the aircraft test centre at Farnborough. In a flash everyone sat up and took notice; they looked expectantly at their squadron commander, Captain Kurt von Greiff, who had to take the decision. After a long pause his eyes came to rest on the wiry little reserve lieutenant, Dr Karl-Heinz Stahl, and minutes later 9K + Ida Henry was airborne with a full bomb-load.

Shortly after take-off Lieut Stahl climbed into the cloud. The Ju 88's engines hummed away monotonously; steadily it gained height. Once they broke out of the top of the cloud, a fantastic view awaited these men. The sea of cloud constantly surged and bubbled, but the four lonely men in Ida Henry had little time or leisure in which to look at this drama which never ceases to stir an airman's heart. They had to concentrate on the task in hand. The French coast lay far astern of the German aircraft; soon they must be over England. The clouds prevented their seeing the ground but on the other hand it stopped the British fighters coming up after the Junkers; that was some comfort.

Lieut Stahl looks at the clock on the instrument panel and pulls his large-scale navigation map of England a bit nearer to have a look at it. Another ten minutes and we'll be there! The tension mounts. Will the British Flak be alert? Senior Warrant Officer Schroeter, the observer/gunner, casts a quick but careful eye over the bomb-release mechanism. The rear gunner, LAC Motes, hunches tensely over his machine-gun. Now we're all ready to go! Ida Henry plunges down through a gap in the clouds. To everyone's astonishment they see below not only the target, Farnborough airfield, but also forty British Spitfires alerted by the radar stations, flying in a tight circle to cover it!

As a welcome some light AA sends up a first, ill-aimed burst. A vic of Spitfires curves in to engage the single solitary bomber. Grimly and calmly, Lieut Stahl makes his run-in, so that Senior Warrant Officer Schroeter can get the target well in his sight. The first bomb is away; and then there are three more little jerks as the others go.

Meanwhile eight Spitfires have dived on Ida Henry. They come in from both sides. Warrant Officer Noemeyer lets fly at them with his first machine-gun bursts. An Englishman fires—spot on target. The bullets rattle into the machine and splinter. A second burst whistles just over Senior Warrant Officer Schroeter's head; luckily he's still lying on his stomach over the bombsight and so escapes death. Warrant Officer Noemeyer is slightly wounded after the British onslaught, but that doesn't stop him answering the Spitfire, which has closed right up to 100 feet, in kind. A hit! The Spitfire rears up, then turns slowly on its side. A burst from LAC Motes does the rest; with a dark plume of smoke it plunges downwards. There's another fighter—up there to port! Lieut Stahl sees what the enemy means to do and with a burst of throttle turns right in on his attacker. Without getting a shot in, the Englishman flashes past, only about five yards clear of the German machine's rudder. It took full throttle and a bit of hard work to get 'Ida Henry' up into the cover of the clouds. Safety at last. But what a state the old crate's in! Instrument panel ripped away, the electrics shot to pieces, the radio smashed and the intercom out of action. The crew is thankful enough still to be able to fly after getting away from that little party.

But the danger is not over yet. After about three minutes flying blind in the cloud the starboard engine suddenly begins to rattle. Lieut Stahl feathers it, and on they fly on one engine. The pilot pushes his foot through the floor trying to stay on course. Soon he gets cramp in his leg and Senior Warrant Officer Schroeter has to get a foot on the rudder pedal to help him. So it is that, slowly, steadily losing height and steering on the emergency compass, they zig-zag their way towards the French coast. And it's high time they landed—they're nearly out of fuel. Suddenly the port engine rattles and cuts out. Silent as a forest. For the last time Lieut Stahl summons up his last ounce of strength and concentrates on making a belly landing—a risky business at the best of times—near Caen. Softly and surely the machine swoops in with no noise but the rush of air, and sits itself gently down. Straight-away every kind of help is rushed to the crew; and ten minutes later they are even being congratulated by the Commanding General, who happens to be in Caen and has watched 'Ida Henry's' forced landing.'

The British radar stations, especially those on the Isle of Wight, had to be taken out to allow the German bomber to fly in with less interference over the English ports. Trials *Gruppe 210* (Rubensdoeffer) led the attack. At about 11.00hrs on August 12th, 1940, *KG 51* with almost 100 Ju 88s, *ZG 2* and *ZG 76* (120 Me 110s) and *JG 53* with 25 Me 109s assembled over the French coast near Cherbourg. Colonel Dr Fisser, commander of *KG 51* and appointed to command this mass formation, waited impatiently for the flights to close up. The main target was Portsmouth Dockyard. Carrying SC250 (550lb) bombs and some SC1000 (1 ton) blockbusters, the *Staffel* leaders headed for their target at 17,000 feet.

On the flight in fighter activity remained slight. It was not until 11.45hrs that they were picked up by the British radar station at Poling. A barrage of 50 balloons came up, suddenly rising to 6,000 feet and heralding an attack. The German fighters tried to draw the British out to battle. The Ju 88 formation split, 70 aircraft turning for Portsmouth. The harbour, the main station, fuel tank depots and small ships were repeatedly engaged from level flight and by dive-bombing. Almost at the same moment 20 Junkers started to attack the radar station at Ventnor, on the southeast tip of the Isle of Wight.

*Flak* began to come up. At 13,000 feet the shooting was indifferent, no more than harassing; but at 7,000 feet and below it was dense and well-placed. More and more bombers broke away, hit by *Flak* or fighters. Thirteen crews from *KG 51* failed to return; At 12.30hrs a Hurricane of No 213 Squadron shot the commander's machine down. Colonel Dr Fisser was killed; his observer, 1st Lieut Luederitz, and Lieut Schad were severely wounded and taken prisoner.

When the formation turned away, Spitfires, Hurricanes and Defiants swooped like hawks on the returning aircraft. Apart from the 13 machines shot down, almost every aircraft was hit by *Flak* or machine-gun fire, in some cases seriously. Major Marienfeld, commanding *III Gruppe*, and 1st Lieut Lange of 9 *Staffel* shot down one Spitfire each. Lieut Unrau and his crew, in 9K + HL, were pursued over the Channel by three Hurricanes. His operator, Warrant Officer Winter, shot one down. One engine of the Junkers was put out and they only just managed to reach the French coast. There the second engine seized and it was by sheer good flying that they achieved a belly landing right on the edge of the shelving coast. They got out unhurt and counted 180 hits on their machine.

Thanks to the early warning provided by their radar stations, British Fighter Command was able to deploy their forces economically but to good effect. On the German side an attempt was made to counter this advantage by raids deeper into the area of operations and by engaging widely dispersed targets. In this way it was hoped to commit all four British Fighter Groups at once. On August 16th the Wing attacked airfields—*I Gruppe* on Redhill, *II Gruppe* on Brooklands and *III Gruppe* on Gatwick; thick fog stopped *III Gruppe* aiming their bombs.

A heavy fighter *Gruppe* from *ZG 26* flew escort from St Aubin, and on the way back engaged opportunity targets in the Eastbourne—Horsham—Worthing area. For once this daylight raid went through without loss. Up to August 25th daylight raids were made on various airfields and on Portsmouth, which we were getting to know fairly well.

Some of the SC250 (550lb) bombs dropped had the new LZZ delay fuse, which set them off hours or days after they were dropped. The new 500lb Flam incendiaries also proved effective.

A few crews had an unpleasant encounter with the 'brook', as the English Channel was condescendingly called. Some could count themselves lucky at being picked up by the Sea Rescue Service.

From this point on fierce engagements at great height became a regular feature as the bombers winged their way doggedly on. Forewarned, the enemy fighters were seldom caught on the ground; they would take off as soon as approaching aircraft were reported, to try as far as possible to catch the German machines on the way in before they dropped their bombs. In the second half of August the Battle of Britain had reached a critical stage for the British. From August 8th on, the Royal Air Force lost 1,115 fighters and 92 bombers against German losses of only 254 fighters and 215 bombers. The aim of achieving air superiority over the island seemed to be within the German grasp. But at the end of August 1940 the bombing tactics changed.

From then on night raids were flown by individual aircraft. At two minute intervals, usually taking off from midnight onwards, all crews who had been trained for night operations—and this was by no means all of them—attacked Liverpool, Birmingham, Manchester and, from September 8th onwards, London. The RAF's night fighter defence, later to prove so formidable, was not particularly effective at this time.

On one of the last missions against Liverpool and Birkenhead, five minutes after its first run, a crew suddenly noticed a flare-up of light from the ground. One after the other, over an area about 3 miles long and 500 or 600 yards wide, innumerable lights appeared; they were supposed to represent a town on fire. The large-scale dummy fire set up by the British south of Liverpool on August 30th, 1940, for instance, simulated burning docks. Many German crews fell for these skilful deceptive measures and dropped their bombs—on the burning hills of Wales.

As a result of the relatively high losses suffered earlier on, new, freshly-trained young crews quickly started to appear in the *Geschwader*. Naturally they were not put straight on to operations. The usual operational training within the bomber *Staffeln* put a heavy load on those who were already flying missions every day. So in August 1940 *Geschwader* Headquarters gave Captain Ritter the job of setting up a reinforcement *Staffel* at Orly, which provided operational training for the newcomers. Night flying was a particular focus of attention. The 7th Airfield Support Company detached a technical platoon under Warrant Officer Weiss to look after their machines.

From the main fighter battle there developed a new phase of the bombing war. On September 3rd, 1940 Goering called the force commanders to the Hague, to discuss a change of targets with them. In his view little advantage was to be had from further attacks on enemy airfields, fighter operations centres, radar stations and aircraft factories. Instead, military targets in and around London would be bombed, on the grounds that the British would only commit their final reserves to protect such a vital target. With the first night raid by German bombers on targets in London, on the night of September 5th, 1940, the Battle of Britain entered a completely new stage; German air operations against the British economic potential had begun.

If the German air operations of Main Battle Phase I had essentially been conducted in support of naval planning for an invasion of England, from September 6th onwards no further connection with the plans for *Operation Sealion* was discernible. This was the beginning of Main Battle Phase II, which lasted until May 10th, 1941. Goering had ordered the opening of operations against the economy at the very point in time when the British fighter arm, in particular its ground organisation and reinforcement situation, was at a nadir and a short continuation of the air offensive against the British fighter infrastructure would have had very serious consequences for Fighter Command.

It is no exaggeration to describe this second phase of the battle as a strategic one. On the afternoon of September 7th Goering stood with Kesselring and Loerzer near Cap Gris Nez on the Channel coast and watched the bomber and fighter formations thunder away over his head. According to radio commentators who were there, he had 'taken over personal command of the *Luftwaffe* in the struggle against England'! 625 bombers in all flew on London, starting in the afternoon and going on late into the night.

About 60 bombers from *KG 51* made raids on London that night, from about 13,000 feet. From a long way off one could see the sky glowing with the fires of the hard-hit city. South of London they found some realistic deception sites. Oddly enough there was very little trouble from Flak. But this state of affairs was soon going to change.

Night after night up to 300 bombers raided London, and the city had no rest. The night-fighters, mainly Blenheims, became more noticable and played on the bomber crews' nerves though they caused no losses in *KG 51*. During this time repeated diversionary raids were being carried out on Plymouth, Portland or Portsmouth; but the focal point of the operations remained London.

The occasional day sorties that had to be flown without fighter escort were nerveracking in the extreme. Quite often up to twenty Spitfires, engaged in a blocking action off the coast, would swoop down on the formation, which always hoped it could take cover in the clouds and 'softly and silently vanish away'. This trick usually served to shake off the enemy fighters, which was just as well. From October onwards *KG 51* flew only by night, or took off so late in autumn and winter dusk that it was dark when it arrived over the target. There was of course no possibility of surprise; the excellent British radar stations picked up the formation almost as soon as it cleared the French coast, and kept track of it with 'the eye that sees through fog and darkness'. By day the fighter-bomber flights of the fighter force, ironically known as 'light Kesselrings', slipped through to their targets; but despite their losses they could inflict no more than a pinprick.

The operations against London remained the centre of effort up to November 14th, but thanks to the tactic of attacking by night there were no significant losses apart from crashes or forced landings on French soil.

*III Gruppe* alone flew a total of 295 sorties in 49 operations. Only nine machines failed to carry out their task, because of weather or technical failures, mainly damaged engines. At a *Geschwader* parade held in the Zeppelin hangar at Orly on November 12th, 1940, Field Marshal Hugo Sperrle decorated battle-hardened men of *KG 51* with the Iron Cross

First or Second Class; many of them stood heavily bandaged, in witness of wounds received in the air fighting.

The target on the night of November 14th was the city of Coventry; the bombers flew in using the *Knickebein* navigational aid, but did not need it because the glow of the burning city showed them the way. The mass attack with 500 tons of high explosive and 30,000 incendiary bombs caused considerable devastation.

During November the *Luftwaffe* delivered further heavy night attacks, on the same pattern as that against Coventry but to less effect, on Birmingham (November 19/20), Southampton (November 23/24), Bristol (November 24/25), and Plymouth and Liverpool (both November 28/29). Along with this, raids on London continued at a reduced scale. In November alone a total of 6,650 tons of bombs were dropped on English cities, and these attacks continued into December.

*KGr 100* and *KG 26* often flew in the pathfinder role, and used flares to lay paths, as they were called, in the target area. These could be seen from a long way off. For in more and more instances had it been found that the radio beacons were being subjected to intensive interference and were useless for navigation. The British were getting cleverer and cleverer at breaking in to our radio-navigation systems.

The *Geschwader* was able to spend New Year's Eve in Paris released from operations, as the bad weather was still preventing mass attacks. In January the effective disruption of the radio-navigation systems, and the activities of British radar-controlled night fighters, finally forced the *Luftwaffe* to switch attacks from industrial centres deep in England to coastal towns, which the bomber crews could find—even at night—without radio aids. This proved to be a decisive success for the British air defence.

In his combat report written after the operation in the night of January 10th, 1941, 1st Lieut Kuechle wrote:

*Combat Report by 1st Lieut Kuechle—Attack by Night Fighters. Mission of night of January 10/11th, 1941.*

We could see the fires in Portsmouth even before we reached Fécamp. We made our run from southeast to northwest. After releasing our bombs at 21.08hrs from altitude 15,500 feet we turned to port on to compass heading 140° for Fécamp. We were flying at 2,100rpm with 11.5 pounds of boost. Over the target there was broken cloud cover at about 3,500 feet, while the Isle of Wight was clear and could easily be seen in the moonlight. Between Portsmouth and the Isle of Wight, about 2–4 minutes after bomb release, the operator reported a night-fighter approaching from starboard at about 90° to our own course. Just before reaching us it pulled up, curved to port and swung on to our tail.

After the night-fighter's first run-in, during which it did not fire, our pilot started to descend at about 600 feet per minute, leaving the autopilot on. Fire was opened at about 100 yards, almost simultaneously by our gunner and the night-fighter. At this the pilot increased the rate of descent and when hits were heard, he dived still more sharply. At 14,000 feet the airspeed indicator was showing 280mph. While in this steep dive the pilot saw the night-fighter's tracer above his aircraft, on his course. He therefore swung off sharply to port. The night-fighter pulled up to port and disappeared.

Immediately there was another attack, this time from below on the starboard side. It was probably a different night-fighter, for the first one could hardly have got into position for a second attack. With the autopilot off and diving steeply, at an indicated airspeed 310mph at 2,300rpm, we turned to starboard with full deflection on the turn indicator onto a southerly course. The flight engineer fired off half a drum of ammunition, and the fighter pulled away.

The radio operator saw a night-fighter above us to port, but it made no move to attack.

Using the autopilot and zigzagging constantly between 180 and 100 degrees, we flew towards Fécamp. We had dropped to altitude 6,500 feet. Since the starboard oil tank was showing empty and the starboard engine was running unevenly, we gained height over the Channel. No one in the crew was wounded. As the hydraulic guages were not reading, the pilot selected flaps and the undercarriage down to test the system; this showed that the main system was unserviceable. We radioed 'Undercarriage damaged, will land last'.

At 22.50hrs, after the undercarriage and flaps had been lowered on the emergency system, we came in to land. On touch-down the machine tried to swing to starboard, but this was checked by full port rudder and brakes. Since it was almost out of control and had such a list to starboard as to suggest that the undercarriage had buckled, the pilot ordered the cockpit hood jettisoned. The aircraft turned slightly to starboard as it drew to a halt. As soon as it stopped, the engines were cut and the electrics switched off, and the crew clambered out.

The aircraft had received 38 hits during the two attacks. The starboard tyre had been shot to pieces. Eight or ten large entry holes indicated the use of explosive rounds from cannon.

(signed) Kuechle
1st Lieut, Headquarters Flight Commander

The *Geschwader* did not take part in the last major operations against England. It flew its last raid in this theatre on March 27th, 1941 against

Cowley near Oxford. For the last time it had a taste of the stinging, accurate British *Flak*.

## Review of Operations and Losses

Before moving on, a review of the operations against England from June 20th, 1940 to March 31st, 1941 is called for. The data quoted are taken from the *III KG/51* war diary, and may be considered representative of all the bomber units involved.

The German Air Force lost 2,265 aircraft, of which 25% were fighters and 35% bombers. These losses appear to have been made good by new production, though it must be questioned whether production kept pace with the enemy's technical achievements. The really damaging losses were however in pilots and crews who had been thoroughly trained in peacetime. These amounted to 3,363 killed and 2,117 wounded, as well as 2,641 airmen who were either missing or taken prisoner by the British. Most of *KG 51*'s dead found their last resting-place in the cemetery at Meaux.

From this point on the German Air Force came to have only secondary importance as an independent arm of the service. Throughout the rest of World War II no further attempt was made to use it for independent operations at strategic or grand-tactical level. Even in a supporting role to the Army and Navy it was no longer able to force a decision at really key points. The limits of German power were revealed, and the time of the blitzkrieg campaigns was past.

*KG 51* AIRCRAFT LOSSES
(OPERATIONS AGAINST ENGLAND)

Period 1 7 1940–31 10 1940 (four months only)

| Damage * | 100% | 70–80% | 45–60% | 25–40% | 15–20% |
|---|---|---|---|---|---|
| Headquarters | 1 | – | – | – | – |
| *I Gruppe* | 13 | 2 | 3 | 12 | 4 |
| *II Gruppe* | 13 | – | 1 | 7 | 4 |
| *III Gruppe* | 12 | 3 | 2 | 7 | 7 |
| Reinforcement *Staffel* | 1 | – | – | 2 | – |

* See note below.

On one day, August 12th, 1940 when the commander Colonel Dr Fisser was killed, aircraft losses amounted to:

| | | |
|---|---|---|
| Headquarters | — | 1 (100%) |
| *III Gruppe* | — | 4 (100%), 1 (30%), 1 (15%) |
| *I Gruppe* | — | 3 (100%), 1 (30%) |
| *II Gruppe* | — | 2 (100%) |

*Note.* Aircraft losses were categorised according to the degree of damage.

| | |
|---|---|
| 100% | Total loss |
| 60–80% | Aircraft unrepairable, some parts reclaimed for use on other aircraft. |
| 45–59% | Aircraft severely damaged, requiring replacement of major assemblies/sections. |
| 40–44% | Aircraft damaged, requiring change of engines or systems (e.g. hydraulics). |
| 25–39% | Damage calling for a complete in-unit inspection. |
| 10–24% | Moderate damage from enemy fire, remediable by minor repairs. |
| under 10% | Light damage, repairable by ground crew. |

*III Gruppe, Kampfgeschwader 51*

Station Wiener Neustadt
March 31st, 1941

*Review of Operations against England from 20 6 40 to 31 3 41*

1 112 missions, 648 sorties, including:

| | |
|---|---|
| Reconnaissance Schwarm | 118 |
| 7 *Staffel* | 205 |
| 8 *Staffel* | 180 |
| 9 *Staffel* | 145 |

2 Flying hours—1,603hrs 31min.

3 Miles flown—26,053,162nm.

4 Bombs dropped—627 tons 600lbs.

5 Losses:

| *Date* | *Tactical No* | *Serial No* | *Place* | *Damage* | *Casualties* * *W.* | *K.* | *PW.* | *M.* |
|---|---|---|---|---|---|---|---|---|
| 13/7/40 | 9K+CR | 7074 | Rouen | Belly-landing, 20% | – | – | – | – |
| 30/7/40 | 9K+ER | 7081 | Nogent le Rotron | Crash, 100% | – | 4 | – | – |
| 31/7/40 | 9K+FT | 7068 | Orly | Belly-landing, 35% | – | – | – | – |
| 9/8/40 | 9K+GS | 7052 | Mondésir | Crashed on take-off, 75% | – | – | – | – |
| 9/8/40 | 9K+DD | 5064 | Mondésir | Crashed on take-off, 50% | – | – | – | – |
| 10/8/40 | 9K+JR | 7071 | Beauvais | Damaged on landing 20% | – | – | – | – |
| 12/8/40 | 9K+ED | 7073 | ? | Fighter attack ? | 1 | – | – | – |
| 12/8/40 | 9K+AT | 5042 | le Havre | Forced landing, 70% | 1 | – | – | – |
| 12/8/40 | 9K+KT | 7091 | Portsmouth | Missing, 100% | – | – | – | 4 |
| 12/8/40 | 9K+FS | 5072 | Portsmouth | Shot down, 100% | – | – | 3 | 1 |
| 12/8/40 | 9K+BS | 4078 | Portsmouth | ? 100% | – | 4 | – | – |
| 12/8/40 | 9K+AS | 5063 | Portsmouth | ? 100% | – | 4 | – | – |
| 19/8/40 | 9K+FR | 7069 | Little Rissington | Missing, 100% | – | 4 | – | – |
| 25/8/40 | 9K+BR | 7072 | Portsmouth | ? 100% | – | 3 | – | – |
| 30/8/40 | 9K+DS | 7076 | Mondésir | Damage on landing, 15% | – | – | – | – |
| 7/9/40 | 9K+CD | 2167 | Villaroche | Damage on landing, 30% | – | – | – | – |
| 12/9/40 | 9K+DT | 5053 | London | Crashed, | – | 2 | – | – |

* Names of casualties are included in the orginal German edition.

| *Date* | *Tactical No* | *Serial No* | *Place* | *Damage* | *Casualties** *W.* | *K.* | *PW.* | *M.* |
|---|---|---|---|---|---|---|---|---|
| 20/9/40 | 9K+MR | 7092 | Lille | Forced landing, 45% | – | – | – | – |
| 25/9/40 | 9K+FR | 4144 | Evreaux | Crashed, 100% | – | 4 | – | – |
| 27/9/40 | 9K+IR | 2174 | Pusscay | Crashed, 100% | – | 4 | – | – |
| 27/9/40 | 9K+BR | 6153 | Oisonville | Crashed, 100% | – | 4 | – | – |
| 10/10/40 | 9K+CD | 2104 | Mondésir | Damage on landing, 25% | – | – | – | – |
| 10/10/40 | 9K+HS | 299 | London | Crashed, 100% | – | – | 4 | – |
| 12/10/40 | 9K+DR | 7075 | Mondésir | Crashed on take-off, 100% | 3 | 1 | – | – |
| 28/10/40 | 9K+MR | 8040 | London | Crashed, 100% | – | – | – | 4 |
| 6/11/40 | 9K+KS | 5070 | London | Crashed, 100% | – | – | – | 4 |
| 18/11/40 | 9K+GR | 7082 | Villeneuve | Crashed, 100% | – | 4 | – | – |
| 18/11/40 | 9K+AT | 7054 | Brétigny | Crashed on landing, 80% | – | – | – | – |
| 20/11/40 | 9K+GT | 7062 | Brétigny | Crashed on landing, 80% | – | – | – | – |
| 31/11/40 | 9K+AB | 5050 | Brétigny | Damaged on landing, 20% | – | – | – | – |
| 31/11/40 | 9K+FS | 3189 | Brétigny | Damaged on landing, 15% | – | – | – | – |
| 21/12/40 | 9K+FT | 296 | Brétigny | Crashed, 100% | – | 4 | – | – |

* Names of casualties are included in the orginal German edition.

| *Date* | *Tactical No* | *Serial No* | *Place* | *Damage* | *Casualties** *W.* | *K.* | *PW.* | *M.* |
|---|---|---|---|---|---|---|---|---|
| 30/12/40 | 9K+LR | 5045 | Brétigny | Crashed on approach, 100% | 1 | 3 | – | – |
| 15/3/41 | 9K+BS | 7119 | Bovoux | Forced landing, 60% | 1 | 3 | – | – |
| 15/3/41 | 9K+HT | 2271 | Bonneville | Crashed on landing, 40% | 4 | – | – | – |
| 21/3/41 | 9K+BR | 6167 | le Havre | Crashed, | – | 4 | – | – |
| 24/3/41 | 9K+KT | 6154 | Villacoublay | Crashed, 100% | – | 4 | – | – |

*Summary*

Aircrew casualties:

| | |
|---|---|
| Killed | 4 officers and 47 NCOs and airmen |
| Missing | 3 officers and 16 NCOs and airmen |
| Taken Prisoner | 2 officers and 5 NCOs and airmen |

Wounded:

| | |
|---|---|
| Severely | 3 officers and 5 NCOs and airmen |
| Slightly | 3 officers and 7 NCOs and airmen |

Aircraft lost/damaged:

| | |
|---|---|
| 100% | 21 |
| 70–80% | 4 |
| 45–60% | 3 |
| 25–40% | 5 |
| 15–20% | 5 |

* Names of casualties are included in the orginal German edition.

Above left/right: The end of the pontoon bridge over the Don at Kalech, used for the supply and reinforcement of Stalingrad.

General von Richthofen singled out *KG 51* for praise when he addressed them at a muster parade at Nikolayev. On the right is the *Geschwader* commander, Major von Friedeburg.

Outside the operations tent at Sarabus, 1942. Left to right: Major Ritter, *I/KG 51* Major von Friedeburg, commander *KG 51*, and Captain von Bibra, commanding *III/KG 51*.

7th (Railway attack) *Staffel KG 51* painted over nose-domes to camouflage this C6 pursuit version of the Ju 88, at the time of operations against Russian railways. The cannon apertures are clearly visible.

Tatsinskaya, 1942. Captain Schoelss (centre) and Major Dierich (right) talk over the results of a mission against Stalingrad.

Groundstaff at Bagerovo, 1943. 1,000lb bombs were towed to the aircraft on sleds. In the background are the Bagerovo radio station and air traffic control centre.

100lb bombs being loaded into the fuselage bays.

An engine change.

Hand-loading SC250 bombs into the external bomb racks.

Zaporoshye, March 1943. The *Geschwader* Commander, Major von Frankenberg-Proschlitz, commends Lieutenant Loeffelbein for the destruction of the Don railway bridge at Ryshkov. Left to right: Captain Haeberlen, Major von Frankenberg-Proschlitz, Lieutenants Winkel and Chiuruski, 1st Lieut Loeffelbein.

Major von Frankenberg-Proschlitz (left) with Captain Rath and Lieutenant Stephan at Bagerovo, May 1943.

The 10,000th operational sortie. The Commander of *KG 51* Lieutenant-Colonel Heize, welcomes the Roesch crew back to Bryansk.

Captain Rudolf Henne (April 12th, 1942), died after the war.

Senior Warrant Officer Albert Spieth (March 24th, 1943), killed at Zaporoshye on October 4th, 1943.

Some of the Knight's Cross holders of *KG 51*.

1st Lieut Eberhard Schaefer (April 8th, 1944), killed at Zamoćs on April 9th, 1944.

Captain Siegfried 'Balbo' Barth (October 2nd, 1942).

While in the II Squadron ops room Major Barth is planning. . . .

. . . operations over the Aegean Sea.

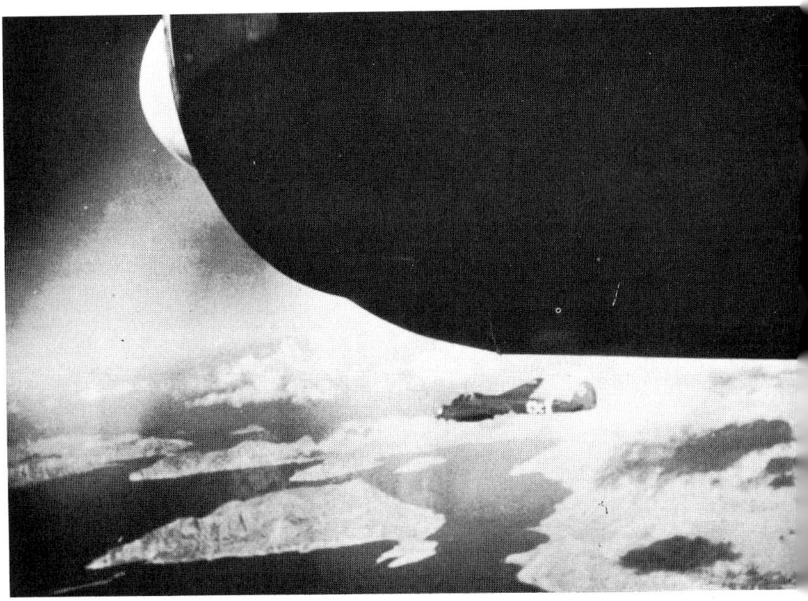

*I* and *III Gruppen* move back to Germany to take over new roles.

Illesheim 1943. A moment's break for *KG 51's* battle-hardened Knight's Cross holders. Left to right: Captain Joseph Schoelz, Captain Klaus Haeberlen, 1st Lieut Dietrich Puttfarken (killed in action April 23rd, 1944).

The first conversion flights on the Me 110 at the heavy-fighter school at Memmingen.

At Illesheim, autumn 1943, before the start of operations with the Me 410. Left to right: Senior Warrant Officers Hogel and Capitain, Captains Haeberlen and Unrau, Senior Warrant Officers Loesel and Puls (extreme right).

Above: Captain Klaus Haeberlen, commander of I *Gruppe* awarded Knight's Cross June 20th, 1943.

Above right: An Me 410 in flight; this was the type used by *KG 51* in operations against England, and during the defence of Southern Germany.

Right: Reichsmarschall Goering talks with Captain Haeberlen at Fels am Wagram.

The Me 410 armed with 210 mm. rocket launchers known as 'pipes', for operations against American 4-engined bombers.

Captain Loeffelbein is awarded the Knight's Cross at Hildesheim on October 3rd, 1943. Left to right: Dr Bahnsen (the MO), Captain Loeffelbein, Major Schoelz (commanding *IV/KG 51*), 1st Lieut Dr Roder (Adjutant).

Lieutenant-Colonel Hanns Heise, commander *KG 51* at St. Georges-Môtel, France, in May 1944.

July 1944. Left to right: Lieutenant Colonel Meister, commander *KG 51* with his adjutant, Captain Sartor, and Captain Grundmann, commanding *II/KG 51*.

A pair of Me 262s of *I/KG 51* taking off from Juvincourt in July 1944, shortly after the Allied landings.

Rheine, September 1944. Right to left: Major Wolfgang Schenck, Senior Warrant Officers Gerd Gittmann and 'Ronny' Lauer, Captain Eberhard Winkel and (back to camera) Senior Warrant Officer Adolf Schwachenwald.

An Me 262 of the Edelweiss *Geschwader* on a rainy evening at Hopsten, 1944.

Major Unrau, commanding *I/KG 51* (centre) debriefs Captain Winkel (right) on an engagement with enemy fighters. But the MO, Dr Denkhaus, had him well strapped-up first.

Critical eyes gaze from the dugout of the ops room at Rheine in autumn 1944. From left to right: Lieutenants Batel, Haefner and Ritter von Rittersheim (killed in action January 14th, 1945), Captain Abrahamczik, Captain Roesch (killed in action November 28th, 1944) and Lieutenant Maser.

The Director of Fighters, General Adolf Galland, discusses with Major Unrau current operational problems with the Me 262 (Rheine, October 8th, 1944).

The last Christmas of the War (1944) at Rheine. Left to right: 1st Lieut Hovestadt, Major Unrau, Quartermaster Hoiss.

Captain Hans Gutzmer, leader of 7 (Railway Attack) *Staffel KG 51*, awarded Knight's Cross February 29th, 1944.

Captain Winkel and Lieutenant Gietmann were killed at Giebelstadt on March 21st, 1945. Senior Warrant Officer Schwachenwald, the radio operator from the Winkel crew, carried Captain Winkel's decorations.

Above: At 15.28hrs on May 8th, 1945, Lieutenant Wilhelm Battel flew in from Zatec and landed in a field near Pommoissel, just by his family farm. (Amateur snapshot)

Top: 'Just like being pushed by an angel,' said General Adolf Galland after his first flight in the Me 262. This is the A2 model with its distinctive figure 13; these figures were usually carried by training aircraft in addition to the tactical sign, for ease of identification. (The swastika was touched out on the original.)

**Flugbetrieb mit "Silber".** Prüf - Nr.

**I. Anlassen.**

1. Selbstschalter für Generator links und rechts, Anlaßzündung und Meßgeräte eindrücken (Achtung bei allen Flugzeugen nicht gleich angeordnet!).
Beim Anlassen mit Außenbord Fernselbstschalter "Aus".
2. Riedelanlasser 3 - 5 Sekunden tupfen, in Tätigkeit bringen, Umdrehungsanzeigegerät auf kleinen Meßbereich schalten.
Bei 800 U. Zündung drücken. Bei 2000 U. Riedelanlasser loslassen, Bedienhebel mit gedrückter Zündung langsam vorschieben, Brandhahn öffnen, Förderpumpen "Ein", Leerlaufsperre einrasten, bei 3000 U. Zündung loslassen.
3. Tankpumpen einschalten.

**II. Nach dem Anlassen.**

1. Fernselbstschalter "Ein". Selbstschalter für Wendehorizont, Flossentrimmung, Staurohrheizung (wenn erforderlich) "Ein".
2. Fu.G. 16 "Ein".
3. Für Sprechverkehr am Platz Raste 3.
4. Wendehorizont auf "Los".

**III. Abbremsen.**

1. Achtung, ob Bremsklötze vorhanden.
2. Jedes Triebwerk einzeln hochfahren.
3. Langsam den Bedienhebel vorschieben, bis 6000 U. (auf Temperatur achten), dann zügig bis Vollast.
4. Bei 8100 U. muß Düsennadel voll ausgefahren sein.(Kontrolle am Gasdifferenzdruck und kann ausgefahrene Düsennadel sehen).
5. Gasdifferenzdruck 0,6 - 0,7.
6. Kraftstoffdruck 60, Schmierstoffdruck 1 - 4, Temperatur nicht über rote Marke.
7. Zügig Bedienhebel zurücknehmen.

**IV. Rollen.**

1. Kabinendach richtig schließen (Achtung, ob Verschlußhebel eingerastet).
2. Langsam Bedienhebel nach vorn, Temperatur beachten, darf nicht über die rote Marke steigen.
3. Langsam gerade anrollen lassen.
4. Kurven mit Bremsen rollen (darauf achten, daß nicht zu langsam gerollt wird, da sonst Schwierigkeiten mit dem Bugrad).
5. Bremsen müssen einwandfrei ziehen (sonst Flugzeug unklar).

**V. Vorbereitung zum Start.**

1. Flugzeug am Start gerade hinstellen.
2. Beide Bremsen betätigen.
3. Flossenstellung je nach Betankung bis 3° kopflastig.
4. Landeklappen auf 20°.
5. Sprechprobe mit Bodenstelle.

**VI. Start.**

1. Stoppuhr drücken.
2. Bedienhebel nach vorn bis 7000 U.
3. Bremsen loslassen, Bedienhebel bis Vollast vorschieben.
4. Anzeigewerte für beide Triebwerke beachten.
5. Steuerknüppel in Normalstellung, Flugzeug rollt gerade aus, bei Abweichen mit Bremsen korrigieren.
6. Bei 180 - 200 km/h Flugzeug vom Boden wegnehmen, nicht zu stark ziehen, da Anstellwinkel zu groß, und kurz wieder nachdrücken.
7. Räder abbremsen.
8. Fahrwerkknopf "Ein" eindrücken, dabei Sperre nach links schieben Knopf springt heraus, wenn Einfahrvorgang beendet. (Fahrt möglichst nicht über 250 km/h beim Fahrwerk einfahren).
9. Drehzahlen auf Reiseflug 8000-8300 U., bei Platzflug 8000 U.
10. Landeklappen "Ein", Fahrt nicht über 350 km/h.
11. Flugzeug in Normallage austrimmen.

**VII. Im Fluge.**

1. Triebwerkinstrumente beachten.
2. Kraftstoffvorrat beachten.
3. Selbstschalterknöpfe überwachen.

**VIII. Vorbereitung zur Landung.**

1. Drehzahlen bis 6500 U. zurücknehmen.
2. Fahrt durch Ziehen vermindern (bis 320 - 350 km/h.)
3. Fahrwerkknopf "Aus" drücken (Achtung, beim Fahrwerk ausfahren wird Flugzeug ruckartig schwanzlastig), nachdrücken 300 km/h halten.
4. Schauzeichen für Fahrwerk und Bugrad müssen aufleuchten "Aus" (da sonst keine weitere Kontrolle).
5. Landeklappen auf 20°.
6. Kurven mit Fahrwerk "Aus" nicht unter 280 km/h.
7. Steuerdrücke durch Trimmen ausgleichen.

**IX. Landung.**

1. Normal Gleitwinkel anschweben.
2. Landeklappe ganz ausfahren, 250 km/h halten, in Platznähe 230 - 220 km/h.
3. Am Platzrand ran an den Boden gehen (Aufsetzen mit 200-180 km/h)
4. Bedienhebel zurück auf Leerlaufstellung (Achtung, nicht auf Stopp zurückziehen, da sonst Orkane brennen).
5. Normal den Knüppel durchziehen, bis Flugzeug aufsetzt. Das Bugrad hochhalten, dabei langsam nach vorn übergehen lassen.
6. Ausrollen, wenn erforderlich bremsen, Landeklappe "Ein".

**X. Verhalten in besonderen Fällen.**

1. Bei Triebwerkausfall Brandhahn zu, Bedienhebel auf Stopp, Förderpumpe aus, mit Seitenrudertrimmung nachtrimmen.
2. Eintriebwerkflug ohne weiteres möglich, kann über laufendes und stehendes Triebwerk kurven, Steigen gut möglich.
3. Eintriebwerklandung ohne weiteres möglich (Achtung, bei links ausgefallenem Triebwerk, Fahrwerk und Landeklappe mit Preßluft ausfahren, Landung normal. Anschweben nicht unter 260 km/h.
4. Durchstarten. Langsam Bedienhebel nach vorn, Fahrwerk einfahren über 300 km/h Landeklappen stufenweise einfahren.
5. Ausstieg. Wenn möglich auf 350 km/h zurückgehen. Kopfhaubenanschluß von Trennstelle lösen, Dach abwerfen, losschnallen. (Die Art des Aussteigens ist jedem Flugzeugführer selbst überlassen)

Pilots of *IV* (Reinforcement) *Gruppe*, *KG 51* used this checklist for first flights in the Me 262. It helped master the novel and complex technique of

Above left/right: Lieutenant-General Josef Kammhuber, the first post-war Inspector of the *Luftwaffe*, who at one time commanded *KG 51*, gave the address at the consecration of the Memorial Chapel at Landsberg on September 30th, 1956.

Below: In 1936 the Hoeschlhof was pulled down to make way for the construction of Landsberg airfield. But its chapel was preserved to serve as a memorial for those killed in action. After the war the chapel had to be completely renovated. Today it is the place where all those connected with the *Geschwader*, young and old alike, foregather on Remembrance Day.

May their sacrifice not be in vain. Let those who survive warn their fellow men of what war brings. (The grave of a crew from *I/KG 51*, whose aircraft crashed in flames on May 23rd, 1942.)

# *IV Yugoslavia and Greece*

On the morning of March 29th, 1941 *KG 51's* aircraft took off from their bases in the Paris area and headed south-eastwards. They flew low over the familiar French countryside. The Vosges, covered by cloud, lay beneath and at Zabernsenke the crews caught their first glimpse of the Rhine. They followed the autobahn from Karlsruhe past Pforzheim, Stuttgart and Ulm and landed for refuelling at Lechfeld where they were looked after by the men of the *IV* (Reinforcement) *Gruppe* stationed there. Thence the route lay over Munich, Rosenheim and Salzburg, and from Linz they flew along the Danube at tree-top height to Vienna. From there they winkled their way to their new station at Wiener-Neustadt not far from the Hungarian border. By evening all aircraft had landed safely. In the surrounding area, in Moellersdorf and other places, the men found comfortable billets. They were astonished to find on the vast airfield a collection of units with every conceivable type of aircraft; indeed, the crews had never seen such a collection of aircraft in one place.

Mussolini, the Italian head of state, had reacted angrily to the despatch of a German 'Military Mission' to Romania when he had entered Greece from his base in Albania on October 28th, 1940. The following day the British responded by occupying Crete—the key to the Eastern Mediterranean.

The Italian offensive ground to a halt almost before it had begun, and was soon under threat from the landing of British land and air forces at the Piraeus and Volos on March 7th, 1941. By March 25th an Italian defeat seemed inevitable.

Meanwhile, at Wiener-Neustadt, *KG 51* was converting to the improved Ju 88 A4. In the marvellous spring weather the crews carried out training flights over the Danube, Lake Neusiedler and the Plattensee, and deep into Hungary and Romania.

On March 27th a military *putsch* in Belgrade fanned the smouldering fire in the Balkans. It was on that day that Hitler issued Directive No. 25. Yugoslavia was to be regarded as hostile, and had to be defeated. The *Geschwader* prepared itself for a new campaign, for the conclusion of a friendship and non-aggression pact between Yugoslavia and the USSR on April 5th had brought the tense situation to a head.

On the eve of the campaign the *KG 51's* aircraft state (all Ju 88s) was as follows:

| *Unit* | *Aircraft Strength* | *Serviceable* | % *Serviceable* |
|---|---|---|---|
| *I Gruppe* | 28 | 17 | 61 |
| *II Gruppe* | 27 | 18 | 67 |
| *III Gruppe* | 23 | 19 | 83 |
| *IV Gruppe* | 10 | 6 | 60 |

Paragraph 3a of the High Command Directive tasked 4 Air Force, under Colonel-General Loehr, as follows:

'As soon as sufficient aircraft are available and the weather situation permits, the Air Force is to destroy the ground organisation of the Yugoslav Air Force *and Belgrade* by continuing attacks by day and night.'

The following extract gives the disposition of the first-line units of *Luftflotte 4* (Vienna) on April 5th, 1941, the eve of the Balkan War:

179 *Luftflotte 4*

German *Luftwaffe* Mission in Bucharest:

*III./JG 52*, Bucharest

XVII Air District Headquarters:
*JG 27* Reinforcement *Staffel*, Gratzendorf
Dive-bomber *Geschwader 2* Reinforcement *Staffel*, Graz

(a) Under direct command of *Luftflotte 4*

4th (long range reconnaissance) *Staffel, 121 Gruppe*, Seyring

*KG 2* Zwoelfaxing (Do 17R)
*I/KG 2* Zwoelfaxing (Do 17R)
*III/KG 2* Zwoelfaxing (Do 17R)
*III/KG 3* Muenchendorf (Do 17R)
*II/KG 4* Aspern (He 111P) (Minelayers)
KG 51 Wr. Neustadt (Ju 88)
I/KG 51 Wr. Neustadt (Ju 88)
II/KG 51 Wr. Neustadt (Ju 88)
III/KG 51 Schwechat (Ju 88)

(b) under the Air Commander Graz, the Commander of Dive-bomber *Geschwader 3*:

HQ *II/JG 54* Graz (Bf 109)
*II Gruppe* Dive-bomber *Geschwader 77* Graz (Ju 87)
HQ Dive-bomber *Geschwader 3* Graz (Ju 87)
*I/JG 27* Graz (Bf 109)

(c) under the Air Commander Arad, the Commander of Dive-bomber *Geschwader 77*

*III/JG 54* Arad

HQ Dive-bomber *Geschwader 77* Arad (Ju 87)
*I*/Dive-bomber *Geschwader 77* Arad (Ju 87)
*III*/Dive-bomber *Geschwader 77* Arad (Ju 87)
*4th Staffel JG 54* Arad (Bf 109)
*I/ZG 26* Szeged (Me 110)
HQ *JG 77* Deta (Bf 109)
*II/JG 77* Deta (Bf 109)
*III/JG 77* Deta (Bf 109)

(d) under *Fliegerkorps VIII*, headquarters Gorna Djumaja

*2nd* (long range reconnaissance) *Staffel, 11 Gruppe* Sofia-Filipovci (Do 17)

HQ Dive-bomber *Geschwader 2* Belica Nord
*I*/Dive-bomber *Geschwader 2* Belica (Ju 87)
*III*/Dive-bomber *Geschwader 2* Belica (Ju 87) and Krainici
*I*/Dive-bomber *Geschwader 3* Belica/(Ju 87)
HQ *JG 27* Belica (Bf 109)
*II/JG 27* Sofia-Vrba (Bf 109)
*III/JG 27* Belica (Bf 109)
*I/LG 2* * *Sofia-Vrazdebna (Bf 109)*
*I/LG 1* * Krumovo (Ju 88)
*II/LG 2* Sofia-Boshuritsche *(2 Staffeln* Bf 109, *1 Staffel* Hs 123)
*7th Staffel LG 2* * Sofia-Vrazdebna (Me 110)
*10th Staffel LG 2* * Krainici (Hs 123)
*II/ZG 26* Krainici-Vrazdebna (Me 110)
*7th* Sea Rescue *Staffel*, Varna
*IV Gruppe*, Transport *Geschwader 1*, Krumovo

Total strength: 8 Bomber *Gruppen*, 7 Dive-bomber *Gruppen*, 8 Fighter *Gruppen* 2 Heavy-fighter *Gruppen*, 1 Close-support *Gruppe*, 3 long-range reconnaissance *Staffeln*

The attacks on Yugoslavia (Operation No. 25) and Greece (Operation *Marita*) opened at 05.15hrs on April 6th, 1941, without an explicit declaration of war, with bombing raids on the government quarter of Belgrade and all major airfields of the Yugoslavian Air Force.

Colonel-General Alexander Loehr, commanding *Luftflotte 4*, himself selected the targets whose destruction would inhibit coherent political and military direction in Yugoslavia. The seat of government, the high command headquarters, the communications network, and purely military installations. In addition he gave explicit orders that only experi-

* *LG—Lehrgeschwader* — a unit normally based at a training establishment for demonstration and exercise purposes.

enced pilots who could be counted on to hit the target would be used, in order to keep the inevitable civilian casualties to a minimum. Loehr went so far as to brief his commanders orally on the orders for the attack since, in accordance with the *Luftwaffe* staff duties of the time, the written order defined the targets to be engaged only by map references.

In the early hours of the morning of April 6th *KG 51*, together with other bomber and fighter units, took off from Wiener-Neustadt and Vienna-Schwechat loaded with incendiary and HE bombs, and flew at 10,500feet in a cloudless sky over Lake Neusiedler and the northern tip of the conspicuous Plattensee lake towards Belgrade. The Yugoslav fighters made a brave and determined effort to protect their capital. Matching the attackers in equipment (with new Me109 fighters they had recently been provided with), but inferior in numbers, they fought stubbornly. The targets stood out distinctive and easily visible. With well-placed bombs the 468 aircraft committed soon had the city shrouded in smoke and flames.*

As German troops advanced, Yugoslav army and air force installations at Novisad, Banyaluka, Gradiska, Mostar and Dubrovnik were also attacked, and in one of these operations Captain Berlin, the Leader of *6th Staffel* was killed with his crew. During these raids the *Geschwader* suffered losses in aircrew wounded. Most of the aircraft came back riddled with holes from enemy flak, or fire from the ground troops.

On April 13th, on Hitler's personal orders, a series of raids was made on Sarajevo. The government was supposed to have moved to the big hotel at Ilidza, just to the west of it. *III Gruppe* alone flew 29 Ju88 sorties on that day, using twenty-eight 1,750lb bombs.

The first phase of this brief campaign ended on April 15th, 1941 with attacks on shipping and jetties in the ports of Dubrovnik and Fort Opus.

The Yugoslav Army surrendered on April 17th, 1941.

## Review of Operations against Yugoslavia

*March 28th – April 15th 1941*

*III./KG 51* — Headquarters, 18.4.41
Ops. Branch — (Wiener-Neustadt)

1 14 missions, 148 sorties:

| | |
|---|---|
| Reconnaissance *Schwarm* | 26 sorties |
| 7 *Staffel* | 45 sorties |

* The author skirts gently round the fact that some seventeen thousand men, women and children died as a result of this attack, which could justifiably be termed the first true terror-bombing attack in history; certainly nothing so far had caused such terrible carnage. In 1947 Colonel-General Loehr was tried by the Yugoslavs for, amongst other things, his part in the attack; he was sentenced to death and executed. AP.

8 *Staffel* 32 sorties
9 *Staffel* 45 sorties

2 Flying hours—482

3 Miles flown—approx. 78,320 nm.

4 Bombs dropped—340,000 lbs., including:

| | |
|---|---|
| 1 Flam 250 | (550 lbs. approx.) |
| 10 AB 36 | (850 lbs.) |
| 9 SC 1000 | (1 ton) |
| 51 SC 500 | (1100 lbs.) |
| 394 SC 250 | (550 lbs.) |
| 170 SD 50 | (110 lbs.) |
| 70 SC 50 | (110 lbs) |
| 24 Flam | (550lbs) |
| 80 AB 36 | (75lbs) |

5 Losses:

(a) In redeployment to Schwechat:
9K + ET, 70% damage
9K + A1, 20% damage
9K + CS, 100% (crew killed and buried at Rastatt)

(b) In redeployment to Wiener-Neustadt)
9K + HR, 35% damage
9K + DT, 25% damage

(c) On operations:
9K + FS, crashed, 100% (1 killed, 2 wounded)
9K + AD, forced landing near Siklos, 30%
9K + AD, forced landing near Bark, 30%
9K + DT, tyre-failure when taxiing, 20%

6 One Hurricane fighter shot down over Mostar on April 12th, 1941 by Warrant Officer Guegel's crew.

Meanwhile, the German advance had pierced the Metaxas Line and fanned out deep into Greece. Athens and Corinth were occupied on April 27th.

Between April 14th and 16th, *I Gruppe* under Captain Hahn had been moved via Arad to Krumovo (near Plovdiv). From Krumovo the *Gruppe*, together with *Lehrgeschwader 1*, was committed to the battle of Greece.

At the same time in Wiener-Neustadt, men of the Airfield Support Company were converting the machines for the close-support role. The large bomb racks were taken out of the bomb-bays, and replaced with the Vemag 90 to take SD2 bombs. The SD2 was a new weapon, as yet relatively unproven, and could be dropped from heights below 100 feet. Wild tales of its effect were going the rounds.

Some crews who were in need of a rest were able to spend a short leave at Marienzell in Steiermark. Others 'flew themselves in' enthusiastically in the still new Ju88s and practised low flying for the close-support role, a new technique for them. *IV. Gruppe* under Captain Stemmler flew into Wiener-Neustadt on April 6th and, drawing experienced crews from all *Gruppen*, prepared for its special training and reinforcement role, so that crews coming fresh from the flying schools could be taught the special tactics and operational procedures without interference from the enemy.

From the tactical viewpoint, four attack profiles were feasible with the Ju 88:

*Horizontal High-Level* The pilot could see the target through the fully transparent nose up to the moment of bomb release, and plan his run-in accordingly. The observer released the bombs using the Lotfe sight* and the automatic release mechanism.

*Low-Level* The pilot made his run-in and released the bombs himself, by means of a button on the joystick.

*Shallow Dive* The pilot aimed at the target using a reflector sight, and flew in a shallow dive, releasing his bombs at a low altitude.

*Dive-Bombing* This technique was similar to the shallow dive but with a steeper angle and from a greater height.

Experienced crews did not of course stick rigidly to these techniques, but adapted their skill and their aircraft's capabilities to the particular tactical situation.

Crews were formally taught only in *IV Gruppe*, and even there they were constantly influenced in discussion with men from the front-line units. Tactical procedures were collated and evaluated, the results being sent off to the bomber schools like the one at Tours.

Although training was resumed, however, Operation Marita was by no means over. The *Geschwader* was mainly employed against the Greek ports—Volos on April 15th, Chalkis on April 19th and 20th and Chania and Crete on April 21st. These raids impeded the British troops in their evacuation from Greece and landing in Crete but the *Flak* from British ships was murderous and the *Geschwader* suffered many casualties.

Armed maritime reconnaissance preceded the German airborne invasion of Crete, to which the British and Greek defenders had withdrawn. Incessant vigilance had to be maintained over the island and the Sea of Crete with the result that crews came back with severe *Flak* damage and, often with wounded, had to put down at some airfield on the way, or even make a forced landing. The cost of each ship sunk in Suda Bay was high.

The maritime reconnaissance operations lasted only two weeks and the *Geschwader* was not required to support the actual airborne invasion

* See Equipment Appendix, pp00

of Crete. Most of the aircraft were handed over to *Lehrgeschwader 1* which stayed at Krumovo, and on May 13th the crews of *KG 51* moved back to Wiener-Neustadt by rail; the staffs were already hatching new plots.

The never-ending problems thrown up by the various moves came out in the war diary of *III/KG 51*. Despite innumerable exercises, something nearly always went wrong. The following is typical.

*III./KG 51*
Technical branch

Headquarters, 18 4 41
(Wiener-Neustadt)

*Report on Experiences of Redeployment*

The operational airfield in question must be thoroughly reconnoitred before the move to determine its suitability and limitations. If this had been done before the move to Parndorf, two subsequent moves would have been avoided and squadron operational readiness in terms of aircraft and equipment would not have been put at risk. This measure would also prevent avoidable damage, such as is caused by soft ground or a field half under water. Further, an ill-organised move of this kind is bound to interfere needlessly with training.

The airfield support companies and the *Gruppe* cannot move at the same time if the move is a long one. If this happens, the *Gruppe* sits on its new airfield without any equipment and, unless a suitable workshop happens to be available, can carry out only minor servicing and repairs. It therefore serves no good purpose for higher headquarters to try and get both airfield support companies on the move at the same time. It would be more to the point to hold one company back until the whole *Gruppe* is airborne.

Movement speed, and hence the speedy regaining of operational readiness, is impaired by the airfield support companies having medium tractors instead of the heavy tractors laid down in the Establishment. If one of these tows two trailers, movement speed is limited to a maximum of 15 mph. Further, the airfield support companies must have an extra truck allotted to them. On their present scales, the loading-space is too small to carry (as for example on the last move) 11 days' rations, which alone take up one whole truck.

The airfield support company must move off in good time, so that at least the dispersal sites and refuelling points have been decided by the time the bombers fly in.

In moving with Ju 88s it pays to take the leading mechanic in the aircraft, and send the rear-gunner in the transport aircraft.

Sub-units must detail off a responsible man to each transport aircraft to supervise both loading and unloading of equipment.

The composition of the advance party should be:- 1 officer, 1 pay-clerk, 4 NCOs and 4 airmen (i.e. 1 NCO and 1 airman per sub-unit).

It is usually not practicable to lay down overall flight serials for the transport aircraft, because this is completely dependent on whether a squadron is allocated enough transports to move in one flight or whether the machines have to make three or more round trips.

The rear party should consist of: 1 officer plus 1 warrant officer per sub-unit.

# *V Russia – The Luftwaff's Verdun*

The preparations for the campaign against the USSR were longer and more complex than those for any other German operation in World War II. The military dispositions for Operation *Barbarossa*, the code name for the Russian Campaign, were to be complete by May 1941.

After the Balkan campaign had delayed assembly by five weeks, Hitler laid down June 22nd, 1941 as the date for the attack. Since January the railways had moved 17,000 trainloads, and during the final phases 106 supply trains per day were added to those. At the beginning of May major formations closed up by night on to the German-Soviet demarcation line. Troop movements on this scale, however well camouflaged, could not remain hidden from the Russians.

The German High Command was fully aware of the vast extent of the front into which they had to penetrate. From the Caucasus to the White Sea it ran for some 2,000 miles, broken by the impassable area of the Pripet Marshes, running for some 375 miles and 125 miles deep between Minsk and Kiev.

The only season favourable for operations was May to October. Before and after this spells of mud impeded major movement. And the difficulties associated with the long Russian winter were also appreciated.

The German armies fielded 145 divisions between the Carpathians and the Baltic, with a further 40 Finnish and Romanian divisions in support. They were faced by 246 Russian divisions.

*Luftflotte 4* had established its operations centre at Rzeszow near Army Group South. Under direct command it had:

- *4th* (long range reconnaissance) *Staffel, 122 Gruppe* (Ju 88)
- Transport *Gruppen 50* and *104* (Ju 52)
- *JG 52* (Bf 109F)
- *Fliegerkorps V* (under Ritter von Greim)
  - *KG 51* (Ju 88)
  - *KG 54* (Ju 88)
  - *KG 55* (He 111)
  - *JG 3* (Bf 109F)
  - *4th* (long range recce) *Staffel, 121 Gruppe* (Ju 88)

*Fliegerkorps IV* (under Pflugbeil)
*KG 27* (He 111)
*JG 77* (Bf 109E)
3rd (long range recce) *Staffel, 121 Gruppe* (Ju 88)
*Flakkorps II* (under Dessloch)

At the end of May 1941, strong advance parties from *KG 51* and from 7 Airfield Support Company entrained at Wiener-Neustadt. They moved via Breclav, Prague and Ostrava to Cracow; and then on East, no one knew where. After three days the men were ordered to detrain and found themselves in a little village station. It took a good hour to unload everything and then they went on by truck. Rain was pouring down. After an uncomfortable night they reached their destination, Lezany near Krosno, at 07.30hrs, 'in the middle of nowhere'.

There were already some huts up and the *Luftwaffe* works companies were plugging away on a runway. The day *KG 51* arrived work began on slit trenches and machine-gun positions. From June 4th, the ground staff started to arrive as passengers on board some of the *I. Gruppe* aircraft. Nobody really knew what was going on, and latrinograms did the rest. Everyone had something new to say over why they were there. Even if the accommodation was on the primitive side, people managed to settle down quite well. Eggs and geese were cheap, and deep frying and roasting was the order of the day in every hut. Water came from a nearby stream. 'Reconnaissance patrols' soon discovered that the Polish-Galician town of Krosno was not too far away.

The days went quickly, filled with preparations for the arrival of the aircraft. By June 20th, just as planned, they were there. But not everything went according to plan; one '88' couldn't get its undercarriage down, belly-landed and stuck at the end of the runway until there was time to clear it away—nothing new!

In the afternoon of June 21st, 1941 the machines were bombed up —for practice, people were told. In the evening everyone went off to their quarters for another round of cards. At 22.00hrs aircrew were brought to red alert. Away with all these diverting drinks, another game was afoot! At midnight on Sunday June 22nd briefing began, and at 02.20hrs the men of the Airfield Support Company were roused. It was in fact around midnight that Captain Bauer, commander of 7 Airfield Support Company, had gathered his men round him, and read out by the light of his torch Hitler's message 'Soldiers of the Eastern Front' which called on every man to give his best. The guessing games of the previous weeks were over at last.

Silent and thoughtful, everyone moved across the field to the dispersal sites. But there was not much more to do; the machines stood poised to go.

The *Gruppe* aircraft state at the opening of the Russian campaign, mainly Ju 88 A4s, was as follows:

| *Gruppe* | *Strength* | *Serviceable* | *% Serviceable* |
|---|---|---|---|
| I | 22 | 22 | 100% |
| II | 36 | 29 | 79% |
| III | 32 | 28 | 88% |
| IV | 15 | 12 | 80% |

Of the total of 1,945 aircraft deployed against Russia (61% of the total aircraft strength of the *Luftwaffe*), 1,400 or 72% were reported serviceable on June 21st, 1941. Thus the aircraft state of *KG 51* was well above the average and this says much for the efforts and the skill of the men in the servicing and repair teams.

At about 03.00hrs the mechanics warmed up the engines. The rise and fall of their note swelled in an ear-splitting crescendo. The crews, still receiving last-minute instructions from their leaders as they walked across, reached their aircraft, donned their parachutes and checked bombs and armament. The sun glowed red in the East at 03.15hrs on June 22nd 1941, when at a single stroke the far-off artillery thundered from horizon to horizon as it opened fire against Russia. The earth shook. The inferno had begun. At about 03.30hrs machine after machine rolled with gathering speed along the grass strips of Krosno and Lezany. Then they were airborne and soon disappeared eastwards. On the roads nearby unending columns of troops ground their way towards the front.

The initial strike was against fully occupied Soviet Air Force bases such as Striyski, Buschov II, Tremblovla, Buctsacts, Chodorov and Lisietshe. In some 80 sorties the *Geschwader* destroyed about 100 Russian aircraft on the ground. The Russian airfields were packed with reconnaissance aircraft, bombers and fighters, drawn up as if on parade, which were later to be seen burnt out round the edges of the fields.

Despite overwhelming superiority the *Geschwader* and the whole *Luftwaffe* took heavy losses from *Flak*, from fighters and, regrettably, from their own bombs. 'Devil's eggs', the five-pound SD 2 splinter bombs, newly off the secret list, were used in quantity. They burst from their clusters like precocious mayfly and rained down. These bombs were developed for use by close-support aircraft against men in the open. Impact-fuzed or set to airburst a few feet above the ground, their splinters carried some 40 feet, with an effect like a medium AA-shell. Dropped in mass, they were bound to produce direct hits.

However, a few out of the 360 small bombs carried by a Ju 88 were apt to jam in the specially designed racks (*Vemags*) in the bomber, the fuzes armed. They would then detonate at the slightest jolt and tear apart the aircraft in the same way as a direct hit from *Flak*.

Many splinter bombs freed themselves on landing, and then burst just behind the machine or lay like insidious time-bombs in its wake. Over and over again the armourers and explosives artificers had to sweep the fields thoroughly, clearing the bombs to one side as if they were lethal bubbles ready to burst at any instant. Despite the success achieved with it in the early days of the Russian campaign, the SD 2 proved to be an unsound development, the more so when the highly effective Russian *Flak* forced the close-support aircraft to fly higher and so prevented its use. Similar problems arose over the similar but larger SD10 bomb, which was too complicated to handle under operational conditions.

The aim was to gain air superiority over the battle-field to cover the rapid advance of the armies, and in particular of the armoured spear-heads, directed on Lemberg and Tarnopol; but the resolute attacks by Russian fighters made this no easy task. On this first day of the campaign four major raids were put in on Russia. All serviceable aircraft took off in the first wave, but seven from *III Gruppe*, including five from *9 Staffel* alone, failed to return. In the evening, after the last aircraft came in at 20.23hrs, the *Geschwader* commander, Lt Col Schulz-Heyn, at his Headquarters in Polanka Castle at Krosno, was faced with a disconcerting balance-sheet.

Sixty aircrew (15 complete crews) were killed or missing; in *III Gruppe* alone 14 aircraft were either unserviceable from damage or had crashed and become a total loss—a 50% attrition rate. In the other *Gruppe* the picture was little more cheerful. The 'old fiddler', 1st Lieut von Wenchowski, *5 Staffel* leader, had also been killed; everyone missed this very popular officer and his racy humour. With feverish haste the machines were put in order, bullet-holes patched over and the remnants of crash-landings cleared away. There was no rest for the workshop platoons of the airfield support companies. Stripped to the waist and bathed in sweat, everybody lent a hand to get the shot-up machines, many of them in bad shape, fit again for the coming day.

About midnight the men dog-tired, collapsed into their bunks. The thoughts of those who had got back safely at the end of the day were simply: 'What about our friends who haven't come back? Let's hope they're still alive. What will tomorrow bring? How will it all end? What will our families at home think? What will the propaganda boys make of it all?' With such thoughts they fell into deep sleep, oblivious of the distant growl of artillery and of the metallic ring of hammers from the workshop area, where work on the machines went on into the early hours.

On this first day the Russians had lost 1,811 aircraft, 322 of them from fighters and *Flak*, and 1,489 on the ground from the *Stukas* and the close-support bombers.

June 23rd was another steaming hot day, and the unaccustomed heat made life difficult for everyone. The rapid succession of missions went on without pause. The armaments teams could not keep up with loading ammunition, so fast was it being used, and everyone who had nothing better to do had to give a hand with filling the belts and drums. Only a fine team-spirit could get the machines ready in time for the next sortie. Despite the high losses—so high that one could almost work out when the *Geschwader* would come to the end of its tether—there was no respite. Old, experienced crews, with many missions against France, England and Yugoslavia under their belts, failed to return. The *Geschwader's* combination of major successes and heavy losses did not stop people wondering whether the game was worth the candle. Many were asking whether the *Luftwaffe* High Command could go on using its modern, two-engined aircraft in the close-support role and accept these high losses of experienced, well-trained crews.

The technical companies were short of essential equipment. Not only was there a lack of cranes and hoists for recovering aircraft which had crash-landed and for engine-changes, but many other tools and spares were in short supply. On June 30th the effective strength of *KG 51* in aircraft and crews was down to one third of establishment. Morale was at a low ebb too, for hitherto the men had been used only to winning. On this same day the SD2 bomb (the 'Devil's Egg') was withdrawn from service. But even after these few days the rapid advance of the ground forces had left Krosno far behind.

On July 4th the formation moved forward to support the fighting round Tarnopol, Shitomir, Kiev and Byelatserkov. Headquarters and *I* and *II Gruppen* went to Luck, and *III Gruppe* to Vlodzimierts.

Russian tank concentrations near Berditshev were attacked with decisive results. The armoured thrust through Vinnitsa on to Uman was nearing its successful conclusion. The crews who had been in it from the start, now flown into the ground with physical and mental exhaustion, were sent back home for a rest. Uncertainty over the fate of missing friends and the high rate of losses had taken heavy toll of their nerves.

On July 12th *KG 51* destroyed the Dnieper bridge at Kanev, putting it permanently out of use and so preventing the Russian forces under Budyenny from intervening with the rapid German thrust.

To everyone's delight, at the beginning of July, the first of those who had made a forced landing behind the enemy lines rejoined their units. Warrant Officer Scheurich's report tells his story in the simple, terse language of the fighting man, not without some dry comments on his escape.

*III. KG 51* Luck, 7.7.1941

Report by Warrant Officer Rudolph Scheurich (9K + HS, 1st Lieut.

Bretschneider's crew) on the attack on Tarnopol airfield, forced landing and escape.

Our mission was to attack Tarnopol airfield. About ten minutes before reaching our allotted target, we spotted an airstrip with 4 or 5 Martin bombers parked on it. We engaged these with SD2 bombs and destroyed them.

After dropping these bombs we were attacked by about four Rata fighters. Their first bursts hit us. The hits must have been in the elevator. The pilot shouted 'Prepare for a forced landing'. The operator jettisoned the hood. Then the pilot lined up for a belly-landing, which went smoothly and we clambered out. Senior Warrant Officer Harenburg pulled the destruct lever, and the machine blew up. The crew stayed together and crept away, moving from cornfield to cornfield.

Just before sunset we were spotted by some Russian military police. They surrounded our hiding place and escape seemed impossible. Three of us put our heads up and tried to give ourselves up.

1st Lieut Bretschneider lay doggo. The military police opened fire on the three of us; Warrant Officer Ober was hit in the head and collapsed. Thereupon Senior Warrant Officer Harenburg and I leapt up and ran out of the cornfield over a potato patch. Harenburg fell down, shouting to me: 'Press on'. I could not make out whether or not he had been hit.

Now the rifle-fire was concentrated on me. After 100 yards I too stumbled, and lay still for a moment. I was fired on again and crawled into a dip with a little stream running through it. I crossed this, and hid in the bog. When things quietened, I had great difficulty in dragging myself out of it.

Navigation was very difficult for I had no compass, no watch and no map. I set out towards the red evening sky. Suddenly I found myself in an artillery position. I sank silently to the ground and crawled back into a cornfield, and stayed there till was dark. Then I leapt up and ran off. The sentry didn't notice a thing.

I had no food with me—I must have lost my ditching emergency ration during the escape. For two days I didn't eat. On the third day I ate some clover flowers, which eased the pangs a bit. On the fourth day I tried clover leaves. I slaked my thirst with water from a puddle, filtering it with my handkerchief. I had such terrible indigestion that I thought I was going to burst, but this got better once I had made myself vomit. Then I became feverish, and began to shake. I didn't think I was going to be able to carry on.

On the fifth day I stopped a woman out in the fields and asked her for a bite of bread. She gave me some. After two or three bites my thirst stopped me eating any more. The woman passed me a bottle of water, and I drank it greedily. Immediately, I was sick again. The woman saw how weak I was and gave me some milk. This time I drank it slowly, and had a bite of bread after each sip. Now I was feeling a bit better. The woman asked me to get out of the field; she was obviously frightened of the Russians.

On the sixth day I thought I should have to give up trying to escape. On a track I met a Ukrainian peasant. He spoke to me in Ukrainian, which I couldn't understand. But when I made clear to him I was a German, he started talking to me in German. He had once served in the Austrian Army. I told him I was an airman on the run and that some of my friends had already been killed. He advised me to give myself up; there were too many Russians around and I'd never get through. He took me with him to his field and hid me there for the day. He dug a hole, I lay down in it and he then covered me with grass. In the evening we went to his house together.

I had hidden my uniform jacket in a bundle of grass, and he carried this on his back. I put on his coat and cap. I also carried the hoe and his lunch-bag. He explained to me that we now had to go through an AA position. As every young Ukrainian had been called up, I had to put on a limp so that I should not look suspicious. When we got to his home, his wife didn't like it much; she was frightened of the Russians too. But when she saw the state I was in she came over to me, and made me understand that I was to sleep in the attic.

There I stayed until I was liberated on July 5th. The peasant folk looked after me well. Another rather better-off woman from the village, who spoke good German, brought a lot of things my way, for my hosts were very poor.

About 11 o'clock on July 5th I heard machine-gun fire in the distance, but it was still Russian. When I thought I heard a German machine-gun, I leapt from my hiding-place and recognised some German armoured cars. Several Ukrainians gathered round me, and soon the whole village had assembled, bringing eggs and milk and wanting to help me.

A German motorcyclist then took me with him to the SS Viking Division, and they took me to Tarnopol. From there, the *Luftwaffe* Liaison Officer sent me to the headquarters of 41 Army Reconnaissance Battalion. . . .'

Reports like these upset the crews. From then on, as they flew eastwards over the front line, they all suffered from a feeling of uncertainty, as if a knife were pointed at their backs ready to strike.

Up to July 19th, the missions were flown in support of the Battle of Kiev within the framework of the advance to the Dnieper. Targets attacked included the Dnieper bridges at Cherkassy, railway junctions near Bakmatsh and Kiev, road bridges near Garnostaipol and troop movements around Novograd, as well as airfields at Nyeshin, Oster and Chernigor. *KG 51* flew without a break; its striking-power was reduced, but now losses had shrunk almost to nothing.

On July 15th *I Gruppe* was transferred to Zilistea near Bacau in Romania, while *III Gruppe* moved back to Wiener-Neustadt for rest and refresher training. The *Geschwader* was split up.

At Tscheschen station the train was surrounded by a thronging mass of people; it must have been the first to come back from the Eastern Front. Gifts were showered on the men. Aircrew and groundstaff were soon off on leave from Wiener-Neustadt. Meanwhile the *Gruppen* were re-equipped with brand-new machines, and fresh young crews rolled in. Soon the *Gruppen* were up to strength. The days of close-support flying were over; *KG 51* was a proper bomber *Geschwader* again.

The elements of *KG 51* stationed in Romania were placed under command of *Fliegerkorps IV* (Pflugbeil) and assigned in support of the Dnieper crossing operations at Barislav. This second largest river of Europe is almost 800 yards wide at that point. Under cover of artillery and an air umbrella, German sappers managed to get a bridge across it. The Barislav pontoon bridge cost many casualties, and must have been the most heavily fought-over pontoon bridge of World War II. But it opened the way to 11 Army's decisive offensive against the Crimea and the Caucasus.

Captain Willi Stemmler, *4th Staffel* leader, who had been missing since the first day of operations over Russia, was still alive! The news was a breath of fresh air for everyone, most of all for the men of his *Staffel*. German mountain infantry had found him deep in Russia and brought him back. Stemmler visited the *Geschwader* at Balti. He still had burns on his face and hands, and looked run-down. The tales of his adventures after his plane crashed over enemy territory, and of the unexpected help he had received from Ukrainian partisans, were spellbinders. It was a miracle that he was still alive. Field Marshall Milch went so far as to pay a special visit to Balti, and have Stemmler recount the experiences of his escape in person.

Lieut Unrau of *3rd Staffel*, with his crew, Warrant Officers Steinbrueckner and Winter and Sergeant Polok, was rammed by a Russian fighter while engaging a Black Sea convoy. His report gives a down-to-earth account of this dramatic flight, and its happy ending.

*Report of Experiences*

Lieut Unrau　　　　In the field, 16 8 41
(Zilistea)

On August 15th, 1941, while attacking a convoy off the west coast of the Crimea, I was engaged by 4 fighters (3 J17s and 1 Rata). The first attack from below by a J17 wounded the rear-gunner, Sergeant Polok, in the leg. The shot entered the aircraft belly through the gap between the machine-gun mounting and the floor armour. Our defensive fire downwards was interrupted by repeated stoppages in the MG 81.

After pulling up at about 2,500 feet and attacking us from behind, the fighter pilot was forced to bale out by well-aimed fire from the radio operator, Warrant Officer Winter. Thereupon, the fighter, now out of control, continued its run-in and rammed my aircraft's tail, carrying away the whole of the starboard elevator and twisting what was left of the port elevator about 20° upwards.

After an initial violent vibration on the elevator, the aircraft became very tail-heavy. Despite pressure on the stick, on which I was also pushing with my feet, the aircraft continued to climb at about 500 ft/sec. with an indicated airspeed of 190 mph. At the same time the aircraft started to slew to port, but I was able to correct this by banking to starboard —without putting a load on the rudder, which was also badly twisted.

After about 30 minutes, by throttling back, I was able to hold a height of 10,000 feet. About 5 minutes before we reached the Romanian coast near Akkerman, the tail twisted again about 20° until it was 40°–50° out of alignment. Expecting the whole tail unit to break right off at any moment, I ordered the crew to prepare to bale out. They stuck maps, first-aid kits etc into their flying suits.

As a light westerly wind was blowing, I tried to head as far westwards as I could. When the impending break-up of the tail, with more bits flying off, made itself felt with violent oscillations and vibrations of the control column, I gave the order to jettison the hood and belly door. I made the crew take their helmets off, to avoid the risk of their getting tangled up. Then the crew baled out through the belly hatch. I climbed on to the radio operator's seat, intending to leave the aircraft the same way. But then the remaining parts of the tail broke off leaving the way out of the top clear, so I went out that way.

After a free-fall of about 20 seconds, I felt . . . free of de-celeration forces and could move easily. Seeing the bits of the tail spinning towards me through the air, I delayed opening my parachute until these had fallen past me; the jerk as the canopy opened was largely absorbed by my lifejacket.

I made a very soft landing; the crew landed after me in about a 1¼ mile square. The peasants who rushed round us were friendly, and some Romanian soldiers who arrived a little later could not have been more helpful.

Summary: If this happened again I would again have the hood as well as the belly-door jettisoned, since this gives the crew much more freedom of movement. The safest way for the crew to leave the aircraft is through the belly aperture, unless—as in this case—the tail is missing, when it seems better to go out over the top.

On August 29th, *III Gruppe*, rested and refreshed, with new machines and crews, flew in to Balti in Bessarabia where they had to rough it in tents. No one was ever likely to forget the plague of mice there; the men ran a book on who could catch and kill the most mice in the shortest time.

Immediately the *Gruppe* was involved in the Army's attacks across and beyond the Dnieper. The targets were concentrated in the area —Kherson-Kakhovka-Melitopol, that is to say on the approaches to the Perekop Isthmus, the gateway to the Crimea.

The reduced strength—*Staffeln* often took off with only three or four aircraft—meant that attacks were mounted in 'penny packets', and were not too successful. Anyone who got away with minor hits or engine damage could, however, put down at Vosnessensk or Pervomaysk on the way back.

Armed reconnaissance sorties were flown against crossroads, communications centres, railway lines and troop convoys. Airfields and AA positions were occasionally allocated as alternative targets. All the principles of air warfare seemed to have been stood on their heads! Nevertheless, losses were at an acceptable level. Early in September *II Gruppe* was pulled out of operations, to be brought up to strength at the maintenance base at Wiener-Neustadt. They stayed in Vienna until the end of November, to complete re-equipment with the Ju 88 A4 and carry out training. They spent a delightful two months training in the wonderful countryside of Semmering and Schneeberg.

On September 10th, *9th Staffel*, under the 'skipper', 1st/Lieut Henne, moved up to Vosnessensk to be better able to get at the Russian armoured trains operating round Perekop.

At last, on the afternoon of September 13th, a major force of 11 Ju 88 A4s formed up over Zilistea to take on the kind of targets proper to formation bombing—Odessa harbour, with its shipping and naval jetty. The heavy, accurate and much-feared Russian *Flak* did not stop anyone from hitting his target or getting home.

The monsoon-like rain of Bessarabia was always flooding the field and the tents, but crews did their best to keep flying. Armed maritime reconnaissance over the Crimea and the bays to the North of it was finally beginning to pay off. Regardless of the weather, groundstaff and aircrew alike put their all into keeping up the continual attacks.

The men of the *Geschwader* were disturbed by the increasingly frequent German Air Ministry reports, of those who had gone missing in the early battles having been found dead. Some of the men had met a merciful end, while—according to what the local inhabitants said—others had been taken prisoner by the Russians and tortured to death.

As a result of the encirclement battle round Kiev, the Soviet High Command tried to pull as many as possible of its troops from Odessa, which was sealed off by 4 (Romanian) Army, into the threatened Crimean Peninsula. This gave rise to regular shipping runs between Odessa and Sevastopol, Ak-Metshed and Yevpatoriya, which now became the foci for air raids.

After the battle of Kiev, Panzer Group Kleist thrust past Zaporoshye and penetrated the Russian defences on the Dnieper. It then swung south towards the Sea of Azov, getting behind two Russian Armies which by October 11th had been finally defeated at Chernigovka between Mariupol (Zhdanov) and Berdyansk. This opened the way to the Crimea.

From October 10th *I Gruppe* was based at Tiraspol, and *9th Staffel* was already forward at Nikolayev. There, on October 19th, occurred one of those incidents which make an airman long to sink into the ground and vanish. Captain Berger was escorting in a lame Ju 88 from *I Gruppe* and telling its pilot what to do. Concentrating on these instructions, he made a perfect landing with his own machine—but unfortunately on its belly! One is reminded of the old airman's saying: 'There are two kinds of pilot—one has already made his landing with the undercarriage up; the other has it still to come.'

Taganrog fell on October 17th and Stalino on the 20th. By October 27th the capture of the Crimea was complete, except for Sevastopol. Far to the north, in front of Moscow, the German troops had ground to a halt through sheer exhaustion.

On October 23rd *III Gruppe* moved up to Nikolayev, where it was joined by the *Geschwader* commander, Colonel Koester, and his Headquarters.

Winter set in. At last the times of grinding through the mud were over, and one could taxi again on the wide Russian runways without sinking in —even if it was bitterly cold. The accommodation, formerly a cadets' block and a pretty Spartan one at that, was lacking in comfort—there were no windowpanes, and no heating of any sort. Continuing falls of snow and biting blizzards turned the country into a snow desert. Servicing had to be done all the time with numb hands. There was no suitable winter-clothing. In spite of the use of Kaerch heaters, the aircraft engines would start reluctantly if at all. The cold-starting procedure never seemed to go quite so well as the theory so confidently laid down in the *Luftwaffe* operating instructions. The mechanics had to start warming up at two o'clock in the morning, to make sure all aircraft would be ready for a dawn take-off.

Partly due to the adverse weather conditions, the Army's operations came virtually to a halt. The capture of Sevastopol was postponed until 1942, in spite of the continuing threat it presented to 11 Army's flank. In December the Russians landed on the Crimea Peninsula at Kerch and established a bridgehead at Feodosia to relieve Sevastopol and, in conjunction with the troops breaking out of the fortress, to recapture the Crimea.

In bad weather the units of *IV Gruppe* flew continuous missions against Sevastopol, Feodosia and Yevpatoriya. Lieut-General Count Sponeck, commanding the German 42 Corps, acted on his own initiative and evacuated Kerch to save his Corps from defeat. This was the first act of military disobedience in the Eastern Campaign. Sponeck, a man of integrity and cool judgment, was court-martialled for it, and executed.

*II Gruppe* moved up to Zaporoshye from its rest area at Wiener-Neustadt on December 4th, and became involved in the battles of Taganrog and Rostov and operations in the Donets basin. Attacks were often pressed home with cloud cover down to 100 feet. The Russian *Flak* played merry hell, and Ratas made repeated harassing attacks on airfields. The *Gruppe* spent the third Christmas of the War, 1941, with no mail but in the company of some Italian airmen. The Don Cossacks sang, but the party never really got off the ground.

In reports of their experiences the medical officers, Dr Denkhaus of *I Gruppe* and Dr Ott of *III Gruppe*, wrote of nervous exhaustion among the aircrew. They mention weeping spasms, and irritability. Shortage of coal made the situation worse, and the winter even harder to bear. Most crews had had no proper leave since the campaign had begun—not even a day off.

Colonel-General Loehr, commander of *Luftflotte 4*, several times singled out *KG 51* for praise in the operations round Rostov. The unit had gained itself a high reputation on the Eastern Front; it had maintained at least two *Gruppen* continuously in operations, and by December 11th, 1941 had already dropped 5,000 tons of bombs on the enemy.

The fighting at Feodosia in early 1942 made it necessary to move *II Gruppe* and *9th Staffel* forward to Zaporoshye. Then, from the beginning of February till the Spring of 1942, *I Gruppe* and *9th Staffel* got a breathing-space. They went to Odessa for refresher training, and to re equip with new aircraft. They handed over their machines to *II Gruppe* and *7th* and *8th Staffel*, whose turn for a rest came on March 27th. This may have been the result of the reports from the medical officers, who pointed out that a thorough rest was essential. This was particularly so in view of the fact that at the time often a *Gruppe* was being called upon to mount only one or two sorties a day. A particular point of discussion was the use of *IV* (Reinforcement) *Gruppe*, which was moved up nearer to the front, to make possible a regular programme of exchanges and reliefs.

The Russian winter offensive forced the German Army to pull back, in the north behind the Volkhov, and in the centre onto the line Orel—Rzhev; and a penetration in the area Vyazma—Smolensk—Vitebsk led to German troops being bottled up at Demyansk. And in the south, after Kerch fell, the Russians broke through near Isyum, Kupyansk and Valuyki, where *KG 51* took part in operations in January 1942. Meanwhile, Hitler had dismissed Field Marshall von Brauchitsch, the Supreme Army Commander, and taken over command of the Army himself.

*I Gruppe* and *7th* and *8th Staffeln* flew repeated missions against Valuyki and Kupyansk, where the Russians, experienced in winter warfare, were trying to develop a pincer movement round Kharkhov. The bomber crews landed at intermediate airfields and received new orders direct from the close air support commander concerned, Colonel-General von Richthofen, so that they could fly three or four sorties per day.

The weather improved in March 1942, but had not yet done its worst. With the onset of the thaw there was 'water, water everywhere' and turned everything into a mud lake. The runway was like a morass. On top of this the Russian 'sewing-machines',* so called because of their engine note, came over almost every night and spoilt people's sleep. These harassing raids often caused casualties.

The strategic aim of the 1942 German offensive was to hit the Russian economy in its sensitive areas, by capturing the Caucasus oilfields and by cutting the Volga at a key point (Stalingrad) to restrict American supplies coming in through Iran. The immediate aim of the German spring offensive in the South was to take Kerch and Sevastopol. As early as February raids had begun on targets in Yushnaya Bay near Sevastopol, at Balaclava, Kerch, Anapa, Novorossisk and other ports in the Caucasus.

On March 14th, 1942 Captain Freiherr Ernst von Bibra, commanding *III Gruppe*, welcomed the famous bomber pilot Captain Baumbach, of *KG 30* who flew into Nikolayev to join in operations against shipping targets off the Crimea. Colonel Peltz had arranged for him to come to the Eastern theatre to pass the fruits of his experience. He flew his first mission on the very next day, taking off for the sea area south of the Crimea, to familiarise himself with local conditions. At the same time the crews which had been sent home for refresher training began to rejoin their depleted *Staffeln* and bring them back up to strength.

On March 18th, Baumbach flew with *KG 51* in an attach on Novorossisk harbour. Very heavy *Flak* forced the crews to jink during their

* 'Sewing machines'—the *Luftwaffe* nick-name for the small U-2 biplanes used by the Red Air Force for night harrassing attacks.

bombing runs, so that the graticule markings of the Lotfe sights could not be held on the target. Crews had to make the best run-in they could, to drop their heavy PC 1000 bombs. The *Flak* coming up from the hills, and from ships in the harbour, was murderous but luckily the bombers escaped unhit.

Captain Baumbach flew his last operation with *KG 51* on March 24th, against Tuapse. He must surely have flown back to Germany with the impression that the *Geschwader* was giving of its best in skill and courage.

The Kerch peninsula was recaptured on May 15th, and 150,000 prisoners taken. Then the focus moved to the battle for Kharkhov, to clear up the penetration the enemy had made at Izyum. Thus the Donets had been regained as a springboard for further operations.

The *Geschwader* was heavily committed to Operation *Fridericus* in the area east of Kharkov. The difficulty in taking the area Izyum—Kupyansk—Voltshansk was simply that the two sides were so tightly interlocked. Then, on May 29th, *KG 51* moved to Kharkov—Voitshenko.

The small wood near Ternovaya and Varvarovka, where a German infantry unit had been stuck for days with some unservicable tanks and had been surrounded, was one of the main centres of the fighting. On May 20th alone, between first light and sunset, one *Gruppe* put in 12 attacks amounting to 46 Ju 88 sorties, and the following day this rose to 13 with a total of 63 sorties. All in all *KG 51* made 294 JU 88 sorties in these two days. A letter from one of the surrounded soldiers tells of operations from the ground troops' point of view, and shows how their will to resist was fortified by the knowledge that they had bomber support:

To our friends of *9th Staffel*, c/o Headquarters L. 37922

At Ternovaya one of you dropped a mess-tin with some cigarettes and your best wishes. So I should like to write to you and thank you from us all for the dash and courage you have shown in supporting us. No doubt you knew the situation we were in. The Russians wanted to squeeze us to death, but they didn't succeed. Your bombs really softened them up. You gave us courage, and we are proud of you. You proved to us what the comradeship of arms is really about, and you kept the pressure on.

We're delighted to be out of the witch's cauldron, but we were nearly at the end of our tether. In those ten days we received practically nothing to eat. Now we're having a bit of a rest to get over it—certainly we need one.

Thank you all again for your much-needed support. Good flying and good luck to *9th Staffel*.

The Russians were broken, and Timoshenko beaten. At Barvenkovo he lost 22 infantry and 7 cavalry divisions; and 14 armoured and mechanised brigades were destroyed. 240,000 Russian soldiers were taken prisoner; 1,250 tanks and 1,026 guns were destroyed or captured. So ended the battle of Kharkov, where the Russians tried to surround the Germans and were themselves surrounded.

The way to Stalingrad lay open. In the space of two weeks, Kerch and Kharkov had fallen and six Soviet armies had been shattered. *KG 51* could put the horrors of the winter behind it.

Now the job was to crack one of the hardest nuts in the world, the fortress of Sevastopol. The five days allotted, and planned in great detail, were to become five weeks.

At this time *I./KG 51* was operating with *Fliegerkorps VIII*, under Colonel-General Wolfram Freiherr von Richthofen. One particular effort of theirs is worth mentioning, because thousands of German soldiers had a grandstand view from the high ground round Severnaya Bay at Sevastopol.

For weeks a raft with 164 AA-guns mounted on it, producing a devastating volume of fire, had been anchored in Severnaya Bay, just near the large lighthouse on Cape Khersonesskiy. It was stopping the German land, sea and air forces from making effective attacks on the strongpoints in the fortress. No matter which way they flew in, from Tiraspol, Kitay or Sarabus, this raft was a thorn in the flesh for the bombers—and a very nasty one at that.

On June 25th, after his *Staffel* had made three previous attacks on it, Captain Fuhrhop, *2nd Staffel* leader, wanted to have one more go at this target. 1st Lieut Ernst Hinrichs was to go with him; the idea was that Hinrichs should drop his bombs to suppress the *Flak*, so that he —Fuhrhop—could go in and take out the raft.

The sun was already going down when they took off from Sarabus. Soon they were over the old Tartar castle of Bakhchisaray and about to plunge into the inferno of Sevastopol. To take advantage of the prevailing westerly wind, Hinrichs ignored the old tactical rule of attacking out of the sun, and flew in from the east low along Severnaya Bay; in the evening light he could see the raft ahead. The Russian *Flak* pounded away at the two; Captain Fuhrhop pulled up and away to dive in second.

Hinrichs dived on his target. The crew were concentrating so hard they did not even notice the tracer flying up at them. On the first run the bombs went in, the AA-raft sank, and the exploding ammunition put paid to it once and for all.

Captain Fuhrhop started his dive, saw what the bombs of the lead aircraft had done and broke off. Colonel-General von Richthofen appears to have been flying nearby in his Fieseler Storch and to have seen this operation. He telephoned the unit as soon as he landed and asked for the name of the pilot, so that he could personally recommend him for the Knight's Cross. And an immediate award of this decoration was duly made to 1st Lieut Hinrichs on July 27th, only a few weeks later. For this reason he never received his German Cross in Gold, which was already on its way to the unit for him. This deed, admittedly helped a little by luck, played a decisive part in the capture of Sevastopol.

Ammunition shortages called for every bomb to be dropped individually, and during the attacks on the fortress this meant for the crews 25-30 dives a day from 11,500 feet to 2,500 feet. It was no mean physical effort in the hot Crimean summer!

With the fall of Sevastopol, 11 Army under von Manstein had completed the capture of the Crimea. Only in the Yaila mountains did a few Russian partisans remain.

Participation in Operation *Wilhelm* to the tune of 300 Ju 88 sorties between June 10th and 13th put the *Geschwader* at full stretch again. The main targets were railway-lines and roads in the Kupyansk—Voltshansk area. On June 28th Army Group South under Field Marshal von Bock moved into the attack from the Kharkov—Kursk area for Contingency Plan Blue (Directive No. 21)—capture of the Volga bend at Stalingrad —and to continue the advance on the Caucasus oilfields.

The offensive began with a thrust towards Voronezh. 6 Army under von Paulus turned south and closed up to the Don west of Stalingrad. Lack of supplies handicapped these operations.

At Zaporoshye on July 4th Major von Friedeburg, II *Gruppe* Commander, took over the *Geschwader* from Colonel Koester, and on July 10th it moved up to Stalino (now Donetsk). From then on the main operations were in support of ground troops and against the Don and Donets bridges.

On July 27th the *Geschwader* was targeted for the first time on Stalingrad. Two days later it completed its 15,000th operational sortie on the Eastern Front, in the course of which it had dropped some 1,800,000 tons of bombs.

Soon afterwards came further calls for support of the advance into the Caucasus. Armavir and Maykop were the targets, and these towns were captured on August 6th. At Kalach an encirclement battle was raging, and there too *KG 51* intervened.

Since August 5th the *Geschwader* had been based at Kerch, to shorten the long flight down to the Caucasus. Only *I Gruppe* continued to fly four and five hour sorties on the northern sector.

Fresh, well-trained crews were flowing steadily into the *Staffeln* from *IV Gruppe,* now at Bobruysk on the Beresina. Captain Stemmler, the

Commander, aided by experienced instructors like Haeberlen and Capesius, taught his young 'rabbits' about the skills required for tactical flying. For battle-inoculation they flew sorties against partisans in the area Kholm—Glinka—Yelnya. From August 8th the targets lay on the Black Sea coast of the Caucasus. These natural harbours—Novorossiysk, Tuapse, Sochi, Sukhumi, Poti and Batumi—were well defended by AA and caused some losses.

On August 15th Ingo Seel and his crew went missing over the Black Sea. Two of the crews (Lieuts Damm and Schwark) sent out to search for him also failed to return.

In recognition of their excellent support, General Lanz, commander of 1 Mountain Division, accorded the Wing permission for all its members to wear the mountain troops' edelweiss in their caps. Naturally this was never written into the Dress Regulations!

On August 16th the *Geschwader* moved via Taganrog to Tatsinskaya, an airfield on the steppes, and four days later resumed intensive operations against the Stalingrad area. *II Gruppe* took over servicing and repair duties from *I* and *III Gruppen* and detached rested crews to them; this went on until September 7th, when *II Gruppe* was pulled back to Stalino (Donetsk) to re equip and operated in the *Luftflotte 1* sector.

Initially Stalingrad was not regarded as a particularly important objective in the summer offensive; the Volga port and the armaments complex at the edge of the city were to be taken out—a target in fact for aircraft and possibly long-range artillery. But after the Soviet 62nd Army was surrounded at Kalach in mid-August, German 6th Army from the west and 4th Panzer Army from the southwest made convergent thrusts onto the Volga bend near Stalingrad. Hitler wanted to see the fall of the city that bore Stalin's name.

The *Geschwader* provided air support for 4th Panzer Army in the land fighting that now started to develop. The air offensive began on August 23rd. In one of these operations Major von Bibra and his crew, Sergeant Moser and Corporals Heyse and Repinski, was hit by flak and had to make a forced-landing at Chir. 1st Lieut Poppenburg of *7th Staffel* saw this and without a moment's hesitation put down just beside it to pick up his friends. Before the Russians . . . could get there, he turned on the taps, and staggered off the steppe which nature had certainly not intended for use as a runway. Von Bibra came down at 11.00hrs. At 16.27hrs he was off again, having changed some of his crew! Up to five sorties that day—cruise, dive, cruise, dive. By evening the stricken city was in flames from edge to edge.

On August 30th 4th Panzer Army broke through the inner defensive ring south of the city. But the attempted encirclement failed; the Russians out on the perimeter knew when to pull out.

'These German airmen,' said the Russian General Chuikov, 'pin everything down.' Good weather and comparatively light and ill-aimed *Flak* made operations easy. The main targets were artillery positions, concentrations of armour, assembly areas and prepared defences; Guamrak, Pitomnik, Gorodiche and Leminsk were the main target areas. Despite the loss of one crew on September 12th casualties remained surprisingly low.

At the end of September *KG 51* said goodbye to the hot, dusty field on the Steppes of Tatsinskaya. Constant dive-bombing had taken the edge off people's fitness and frayed their nerves. Gastroenteritis and dysentery, caused by poor rations and unhygienic accommodation were daily problems. The unit now moved into a rest area at Sarabus, in the gentle surroundings of the Crimea.

On September 21st, *II Gruppe*, having re equipped at Stalino (Donetsk), moved to Bobruysk to join *IV Gruppe*; they remained there under *Luftflatte 1* until October 5th.

Few will forget the days spent in the Crimea. Splendid joyrides round the lovely peninsula without any interference from the enemy, excursions to the Tartar castle at Bakhchisaray and to Sevastopol, or a long, hard walk in the hills past vineyards hanging heavy with grapes—all this did the men good and got them relaxed, even if they were a long way from their families and all the problems back at home. Unit spirit had always remained exceptional and a source of strength; It was not war as such which welded this, but simply being thrown together in the daily routine. Who has ever used or can ever use the comradeship of arms to solve political problems? This unsentimental comradeship is something that no one can understand without himself experiencing it.

In the period from October 25th to November 5th, 1942, *II Gruppe* moved to Armavir without groundstaff, except for leading mechanics. From there they flew missions against Ordzhonikidze (Dzandzhikau), Chegem I and II, Nalchik and Tuapse.

About ten o'clock in the evening on November 4th, one of the Russian harassing bombers happened to drop a light bomb into the fuel dump at the edge of Armavir airfield. There was a flash, and the flames spread to the fuelled and bombed-up aircraft. Since the field had several units on it, and was packed with more than a hundred Ju 88s and He 111s, there was no lack of combustible material. Only one of the *II Gruppe* aircraft survived without damage. The unit was forced to move back to Bagerovo on the Kerch peninsula, to get a new set of aircraft.

The rest did not last long, and on November 3rd the *Gruppe* back at Tatsinskaya. Cold, snow and a violent, icy wind made life in the dugouts difficult; the temperature often dropped to zero, and sometimes as low as minus 30°F. The technical side had a particularly hard time of it; they had to get up in the middle of the night to shovel the snow away from the aircraft and warm them up. Frostbite was especially common among the technicians, who had to check radios, bomb-release mechanisms and engines, tasks which could not be done in thick gloves. The guns froze up, oil froze solid and the situation was desperate.

Every day the *Geschwader* was named in the communiqués on the battle of Stalingrad. Every night the Russians made harassing raids, which got on everyone's nerves and caused casualties.

Major 'Fritze' Dierich was commanding *I Gruppe* at Tatsinskaya, and had elements of *III Gruppe* under him. When Colonel Conrady crashed, he took over command of the *Geschwader* until Major von Frankenberg-Proschlitz arrived on February 5th 1943.

One factor made an important contribution to morale: by synchronising transmission times, the radio technicians were always able to establish communication with a station back home. Every now and then a Ju 88 in Russia would climb high, wind out its trailing aerial and make contact with the radio station in Berlin, to pass messages including some carefully veiled private ones. Thus Dr Rumbaum, the *Geschwader* meteorologist, was informed of the birth of a daughter in the following terms:

'TOPSEC. Restricted Access For Dr Rumbaum. New tail-less aircraft type fit for take-off, production plant ready to accept further work.'

The Soviet army groups Southwest (Valutin), Don (Rokossovski) and Stalingrad (Yeremenko) broke through the sector held by Romanian 3rd and 4th Armies, flanking the German 6th Army to the left and right, and at 16.00hrs on November 22nd, at the Don bend near Kalach, they closed the pincers behind the 6th Army under Paulus. A total of 284,000 men of the 6th Army, and elements of the 4th Panzer Army, were caught in the trap.

Hitler vetoed the proposed break-out because Goering, misjudging the actual situation, promised that the *Luftwaffe* would supply the surrounded troops.

Things had come to a halt on the Caucasus front.

By December 7th the *Geschwader* and its Headquarters at last found themselves back in permanent accommodation in Rostov. The cold dugouts at Tatsinskaya had got everybody down. Airmen can take it, but the living conditions and airfield facilities at 'Tatsi' were too much. Operational efficiency was suffering. And in any event the field was needed for the air transport units asigned to the Stalingrad air-lift.

Christmas was near, but there was little Christmas spirit; many were spending their fourth Christmas in the field.

From Tatsinskaya came the news that the airfield had been attacked and overrun by Russian armoured spearheads on the morning of

Christmas Eve, when General Fiebig and his headquarters were still there. In appalling weather and in the face of every kind of difficulty most of the aircraft were flown out to Rostov-West and Taganrog—with 500 yards visibility and cloud down to 100 feet! *KG 51* had had another lucky escape. German troops retook Tatsinskaya a few days later.

*Geschwader* Headquarters made a three-day trip by road to collect the Christmas mail from Sarabus and bring it to Rostov. But this was about all that the commander could do for the morale of his men.

One day was like another—no celebrations, no Christmas. War! Despite the prevalence of fog, the *Geschwader* flew covering missions against the Don bend. On Christmas Eve the aircrew gathered in the mess at Rostov to sample the presents from the unit canteen—one fruit cake, 50 cigarettes, razor-blades, red wine and toothpaste. But this pleased everyone and in a strange way even made them feel happy.

A lot of Christmas mail was still missing; throughout the theatre the transport resources were needed for other more important things. The crews shared out the marzipan loaves and gingerbread, now hard as a rock, which had come from home.

1st Lieut Ernst Hinrich's crew, of *2nd Staffel*, was in particularly good form that evening. They had been shot down beyond the line and reported missing. The casualty list was read out on the radio on December 23rd, when they were already back with their unit. Thanks to help from the highest quarters these men were able to speak to their parents, wives or fiancées before Christmas. In fact it was nothing unusual for aircrew to be reported missing or killed in the papers back at home when in fact, after a rugged trek through the enemy lines, they had already rejoined their units.

Army Group Don under von Manstein tried to relieve Stalingrad from the southwest with Hoth's 4th Panzer Army. They got to within 30 miles of the city, but when the Soviet offensive on the Don opened up the Italian 8th Army sector, the relief attempt had to be abandoned.

The *Geschwader* had the depressing task of dropping leaflets onto the Romanian forces, in an attempt to stop their panic-stricken flight and make them stand and fight. But to no avail!

Cold, bad weather and serious logistic problems faced those engaged in the Stalingrad air-lift with utterly insupportable difficulties.

The Russians, their troops hardened to the winter, pressed vigorously forward to the lower Chir and the Donets. There could be no relief or reinforcement of the southern front, for German forces in the north and the centre were also engaged in heavy fighting.

Colonel Conrady arrived at Rostov on January 3rd 1943 to take over the *Geschwader* from Major von Friedeburg. He quickly won the confidence of his men; everyone respected him both as a commander and as an airman. But only five days later he failed to return from an operation against the Baskunchak railway junction on the main supply line to Stalingrad. Against all the rules, he had made another circuit over the target to observe the hits. He was caught by *Flak* and crashed in flames with his crew.

That day started an extraordinary run of bad luck for *KG 51*. I *Gruppe* alone lost thirteen crews in three days. When the weather cleared, new fighting flared up round Elista, in the broad snowscapes of the Kalmukh Steppes.

Sergeant Schwachenwald, operator to Captain Winkel who was later to lead *3rd Staffel*, made this report:

'Under us an endless crocodile of Romanians was flooding back. Our operations were successful, but generally speaking useless, because they were mostly just isolated engagements of Russian troops following up. Here in front of Rostov we were experiencing war with the odds against us. Everything went wrong, nothing clicked any more. We were short of bombs, sets, spares and fuel for our aircraft. There was no heating in the billets and it was miserably cold; we burnt everything we could lay our hands on—door-frames, tables and chairs—to stop ourselves freezing to death.'

In January 1943, while Edelweiss *Geschwader* was playing a leading role in support of the withdrawal from the Maykop—Krasnodar sector into the Taman Peninsula, the struggle for Stalingrad was nearing its end. Appalling losses, freezing cold and hunger wore down the strength of the defence, despite heroic resistance in day upon day of house-to-house fighting. Many of the supply containers they so badly needed were lost as the ring tightened and they fell into Russian hands.

On January 31st Field Marshal Paulus surrendered, and on February 2nd all fighting ceased. The word Stalingrad had come to stand for a defeat without equal.

The last elements of the airfield support companies got clear of Rostov, taking technical equipment of *KG 51* with them, on February 5th just as Russian tanks were already on the edge of the field. The saving of this precious equipment must count as one of the technicians' greatest achievements. A German engineer unit had been ordered to blow up the station at Sapadny, west of Rostov, although the train—with no engine—was standing ready. There was barely an hour to go. The bulk of the ground-staff managed to find an army train and pulled out. But 1st Lieut Feldmann with a party of twenty volunteers refused to give up. Two of their own canteen trucks were quickly cleared, and the alcohol worked wonders with the railway staff. By a lucky chance Feldmann was able to get through on the telephone to Taganrog and demand an extra engine. This arrived at the last moment and pulled the train out;

they were hardly clear of the station when it went up. The sappers had a precise timetable to work to. Thanks to the determination of a small bunch of men, the *Geschwader* still had its key specialists and its technical equipment.

In the confusion of evacuating Rostov and moving to Zaporoshye, *I Gruppe* lost its popular and dashing *3 Staffel* Leader, Captain Georg Holle, Knight's Cross. He went missing on a meteorological and reconnaissance sortie on February 27th, presumably hit by *Flak*.

As a result of the course the ground operations were now taking, the *Geschwader* moved back once more to Zaporoshye. *II Gruppe* handed over their aircraft to *I* and *III Gruppe*, and were pulled out for rest and refresher training. In this phase of the campaign in the East, when the Russians were massing their *Flak* at almost every key point, many a sortie ended with the aircraft shot-up lying in the deep snow of the Russian countryside. Quite often the leader of a pair would land beside his crippled wingman and pick up the crew, a dashing way of getting them out of a unpleasant predicament. Jochen Schulze, the war correspondent, wrote up the 201st operational mission of Lieut Winkel and his crew. They made a bold rescue of this kind in enemy territory, saving Lieut Geruschke and Sergeants Floegel, Silberbauer and Broeggelwirt.

With hits in both engines, Lieut Geruschke had had to put down with his crew. What would happen? Would they manage to break through? The first thing to do was to get away from the aircraft. Russian soldiers were already hot on their heels, as they were trying to get to a railway embankment for cover. From above Lieut Winkel could see that they were heading straight for a village full of Russian tanks. With his usual calm, Lieut Winkel went in. He dropped his bombs on the village, landed in the snow in an open field, and taxied after his friends, throwing up a long plume of snow behind him. Sergeant Schwachenwald, the observer, kept the Russians' heads down with his machine-gun, helped by the radio operator, Sergeant Sicker. In a flash the gunner, Sergeant Ziemann, had the belly-blister open and helped the exhausted Lieut Geruschke on board. The others clambered hurriedly into the bomb-bay, knowing that the doors were held closed only by springs! Its engines screaming, Winkel's Ju 88 heaved itself off the ground. It flew just over the heads of the astonished Russian tank crews, who threw up everything they had as if they hoped to kill two birds with one stone. But both crews got safely home—four friends, a whole precious crew, had been rescued.

A month earlier, on January 27th, Lieut Geruschke had plucked 1st Lieut Bayer and his crew, out of a similar situation south of Rostov Bataysk by a landing in no-man's-land.

On February 21st Russian armoured spearheads pushed right forward to Alexandrovka, only a few miles north of Kirovograd, and had shot up a German railway train.

Back at Zaporoshye *I Gruppe* Commander, Captain Claus Haeberlen, did not hesitate. Without waiting to put higher headquarters in the picture, he ordered his squadron onto this target. Relentlessly, with up to seven sorties in the day, this wedge of Russian armour which had penetrated deeply without being spotted was pounded to destruction. The official order from *Fliegerkorps* arrived just as the *Gruppe* report of successful completion was being prepared. On the following day, February 22nd, the targets were Russian tanks just to the east of Zaporoshye —only 10 miles from the airfield. This threat too was dealt with. Hitler had arrived on February 17th at Manstein's headquarters in Zaporoshye, to investigate on the spot the 'disobedience' of Hausser's SS Armoured Corps, which had evacuated Kharkov on 15th February against Hitler's orders. Manstein gave him the operational briefing. On learning how near the Russian tanks were, Hitler was into his FW 200 'Condor' and off like a bat out of hell. Manstein now had a free hand to put the dangerous situation to rights. A series of cool and bold mobile operations between the Dnieper and the Donetz smashed the Russian 6th Army and Tank Group Popov. Manstein's Corps prepared for the attack on Kharkov.

Until Kharkov was retaken on March 15th 1943—in fact by Hausser's Panzer Group—*I Gruppe* was engaged continuously in support. Balaklaya, Isyum and Kupyansk were the targets—the crews knew them already from the days of the first rapid advances.

*III Gruppe* on the other hand was in action over the Manych and the Caucasus, where Stalin, with a super-Stalingrad in mind, wanted to break the south wing of the German Army. He tried to close the gateway to the Caucasus at Rostov; Badenov's armoured spearhead overran Tatsinskaya—but got its own head in the noose, and was destroyed. The Russian bridgehead at Manychskaya was wiped out, and Rostov remained open for the withdrawal of German troops from the Caucasus. 1st Panzer Army was able to secure the Don crossings at Rostov, while 17th Army was holding the 'Gothic Line' on the Kuban against very heavy Russian pressure.

At Mineralnye Vody, Armavir, Kropotkin and Krasnodar troop concentrations, artillery and rail targets had to be engaged—key points on which, as so often, the *Geschwader* was committed. The men of *KG 51* were used to this fire-brigade role. Throughout, 7 (Railway Attack) *Staffel* with its fighter version of the Ju 88, the C6, specialised on railway targets.

From February 27th, 1943 the *Geschwader* was in the eastern Crimea, at Bagerovo on the Kerch Peninsula. Major Egbert von Frankenberg und Proschlitz—today a defence expert in East Germany

—commanded it, with *I Gruppe* at Zaporoshye under Major Haeberlen and *III Gruppe* at Bagerovo under Major Rath.

The SD-2 splinter bomb, the 'Devil's Egg' of such mixed repute, had now been modified so that it could be effectively dropped from greater heights using a new magazine.

The recitation below was given in the mess at Kerch by Major Dr Kupfer, commander of a dive-bomber wing. This parody, exaggerated though it may be, gives an idea of how the German bomber crews were feeling and thinking at this time.

*Triumphal Entry through the Brandenburg Gate, 1961*

175 Air Force bands march by with rousing tones. Then there's a long gap. With measured tread, decked out in gold from head to foot, the Marshal of the World goes by. The Marshal of the Hemisphere follows and then, after another gap of a mile or more, the Marshal of the Underworld. Then the people break into cheers. The star-clustered darlings of the German people, the fighter pilots, march past, pushing in front of them the Giant's Cross to the Knight's Cross of the Iron Cross on its self-propelled mounting.

Another long gap. Then come 25 Marshals of the Nation, all under 30, in their sleek white uniforms. Then a small boy with a banner which says: 'I am the advance party of the rear party, forgotten in Greece.'

There follows an old lady, bowed in grief and supported by the appropriate Party dignitaries; she is the widow of the last long-range reconnaissance pilot. Then a grey-haired man, his face furrowed deep with care, a brief case under his arm and in it a Top Secret telegram: 'My grateful recognition to the bomber crews'.

And then the crowd freezes and there appears a cart drawn by four white horses, and on it a cage, and in the cage a man in chains, and round him eight attendants, each with a placard: 'Warning. Do not excite. Public danger.' And he is the last surviving dive-bomber pilot, and had served in every theatre.

Tanned brown and bearing their victories lightly, the staff-officers march through the Brandenburg Gate. As usual the technical personnel were unable to take part in the parade, as they had not been told about it in time.'

On April 19th, 1943 *I Gruppe* moved via Zaporoshye to Poltava, destined for a new role back in Germany.

During that month, despite enormous losses, the German army, protected by the spring thaw, was able to re-establish a coherent front in the East. On the Kursk sector, an almost rectangular westward salient gave cause to fear that the Russians would launch a further offensive. Hitler refused to straighten the curve in the front, and later decided to launch his offensive there under the codename Operation Citadel.

Up to the end of May 1943 *III Gruppe* remained under Air Headquarters Crimea (Colonel Bormann) and achieved several mentions in communiqués for its operations in the northern Caucasus. Then its commander, Major Rath, and Major Voss with *II Gruppe* brought their units to join the *Geschwader* Headquarters at Bryansk.

On April 8th, and the *Geschwader* commander, Major Ernst von Frankenberg und Proschlitz with his crew (observer Fischbacher, radio operator Miehe and gunner Hain) failed to return. He, his crew, and the *Geschwader* operations officer with all his papers, strayed over the Russian lines and were shot down or had to make a forced landing. The next evening von Frankenberg's voice was on Radio Moscow! Later in Krasnogorsk, Zone 1, he belonged to an 'Action Group' in the 'League of German Officers'. Previously he had always talked like Goebbels making a propaganda speech; with equal facility he now took to the line of his new masters in Moscow.

Lieut Colonel Hanns Heise took over the *Geschwader* in Bryansk. By May 10th, 1943 *II* and *III Gruppen* were flying missions in the Kursk area against railway stations and supply dumps, and their losses were relatively light. Mass night raids by several *Geschwader* were made on 2nd June, on the tank factories and foundries in Gorki, to the east of Moscow. The crews had to fly up to five hours over enemy territory by night. The operation was led by Major General Buelowius of 1st *Fliegerdivision*. Five raids of this kind, each of about 100 aircraft, crippled Russian tank production at Gorki for a month or two. The chemical complex at Yaroslav, north of Moscow, suffered the same fate on the night of June 20th.

From the end of June *KG 51* was engaged in supporting the Army in the Kursk-Orel area, in preparation for the great Operation Citadel. This powerful two-phased battle, the largest and most decisive of the war against Russia, opened at 03.30hrs. on July 5th 1943 with a strike by 1,700 bombers, dive-bombers, fighters and close-support aircraft on airfields, strong-points and artillery positions. Despite numerous isolated successes—such as the destruction of complete Soviet tank brigades from the air—the operation did not achieve its aim; the enemy was too strong. On 17th July the attack had to be broken off; Soviet military historians are right to call this 'the battle that shaped the history of the world', for it was this and not Stalingrad which marked the turning-point of the war. The German Army reserves melted away in this battle, and German offensive capability was broken once and for all.

On July 12th at Bryansk *III Gruppe* had flown its 10,000th. operational sortie. A fortnight later the *Geschwader* Headquarters with *II* and *III Gruppe* moved to Seshchinskaya near Roslavl. The *Gruppe* lost many crews here from partisan activity. The partisans had dispersed themselves round the Russian Countryside, and used to come out at night and attach charges with barometric fuzes to the aft 250 gallon tanks of the Ju 88s, which stood ready fuelled and bombed-up. On sudden loss of height, as for example in a dive-bombing attack, these charges went off and blew the machines to pieces in the air. At first everyone was puzzled but then, in the course of a security check of the airfield, an innocent-looking Russian peasant woman was found with a basket of eggs in which was hidden a charge fitted with magnetic attachment plates.

After the collapse of the central sector of the front, the *Geschwader* moved south, on August 10th, to Kirovograd, where the southern front had become fluid. Novorossiysk fell; and only in the Crimea did the 17th Army under Colonel-General Jaenecke hold firm. At Kremenchug a Russian salient formed, pointing towards Kirovograd and Krivoy Rog. Uninterrupted sorties had to be flown to support the ground forces, and this soon forced a move to Poltava and Kiev.

Finally, on September 7th, Headquarters *KG 51* and *III Gruppe* moved back home to convert to the Me 410 at Illesheim. But *II Gruppe* was assigned to yet another special role in Southeast Europe.

On September 19th, and Major Voss and his *II Gruppe* transferred at short notice to Salonika. What had happened?

On September 8th Marshal Badoglio, the new Italian prime minister, had signed a separate armistice with the Allies, who had landed in Sicily. Since 1941 the Italians had been responsible for Greece. Small detachments of British troops had landed on the islands of Leros, Kios, Samos and Kos. These islands were to be retaken and air support was required for the German landings. In addition to attacks on the islands, shipping targets were engaged off Cyprus and south of Crete.

*II Gruppe* chalked up its 13,000th operational sortie at Salonika on November 14th, it had dropped 200,000 tons of bombs.

Armed reconnaissance sorties were flown in the Dodecanese area, to look for enemy warships which were said to be putting men and supplies ashore on the islands at night. British cruisers and destroyers were priority targets; but they seemed to disappear from view as if at the wave of a wand. Strip by strip the bomber crews searched for the enemy in hours of hard, relentless flying. The men of *II/KG 51* had to peer into hundreds of inlets, tucked away in the islands, until at last they found the enemy.

On Sunday November 22nd six Ju 88s took off from Salonika at 15.00hrs, on the 'island round tour'. Soon after they were airborne, bad visibility forced the formation to split up. But Moser, Schaper and Winkler stayed together. From Rhodes they probed their way towards

Castellorizo, and then in the direction of Cyprus. Nothing was seen. On the way back they set a diagonal course between Africa and Crete to continue their search. Suddenly, off Leros, the ships they had sought for so long were beneath them: two cruisers and two destroyers, cutting through the sea at full speed and churning out long white wakes. Hans Moser's aircraft was flying a little ahead of the others and was in the best position for an attack. He chose the largest 'tub' and glided in to drop his bombs at low level. As the other aircraft closed on the cruisers, the *Flak* started; every machine suffered splinter-hits. But they dived on a cruiser and Moser's crew scored direct hits. Two 1 ton bombs had hit the cruiser, and she turned through 90° almost in her own length and made off hidden in black smoke and leaving a long trail of oil. On the way back three Beaufighters attacked the formation, but failed to achieve anything; Schaper's crew hit one, and it plunged blazing into the sea. Everyone landed safely at Salonika at 17.30hrs.

On November 20th *II Gruppe* was off back to Russia. Major Barth took over the unit from Major Voss. They moved to Kalinovka to support the encirclement battle at Cherkassy, then to Vinniza against the Russian thrust near Fastor and Shitomir, and thence to Lublin. Finally, in the following Spring, they too came back to Hildesheim for conversion to the Me 410.

According to the available records, the *KG 51* lost 703 men in all during the Russian Campaign, 146 officers, 416 senior ranks and 141 airmen.

# VI Home Air Defence and Strikes Against England

The year 1943 saw the German armies in retreat on all fronts. Hitler, it is true, coined the concept 'Fortress Europe'; but unfortunately he had forgotten about putting a roof on his fortress. Home air defence had been neglected. The catastrophe of Hamburg, in July 1943, finally provided the impetus for strengthening of the fighter force. To this end *KG 51* was ordered to convert to the new Me 410 Hornet bomber destroyer, which could carry four 210mm rockets. The *Gruppen* were to re-assemble at Illesheim and Hildesheim.

Adolf Schwachenwald wrote in his diary of the flight back home.

'All *I Gruppe* crews were infected with the sense of great expectations that greeted our move back home. After two years of the war in Russia and continuous commitment in almost every theatre, the excitement was understandable. The machines were stuffed to bursting-point with our luggage and gear, and in our hearts we were more than ready to say goodbye to Russia.

We flew towards the German frontier at about 10,000 feet in two groups of 6–8 aircraft each. We wanted to make the most of our deep-felt delight at crossing the frontier by making something of a spectacle of it. So just short of the Polish–German frontier we changed into open low-level formation. It was wonderful beyond all words, this homecoming! Over the border countryside we flew, firing our machine-guns into the air in a *feu de joie*. Below us people took fright and dived for cover, sensing danger in our outburst of happiness. After flying low for a few minutes the formation climbed to cruising height and closed up to make the rest of the flight to our destination airfields a well-disciplined one.

At about 14.08hrs we all touched down smoothly at Illesheim near Nuernberg. With an intermediate stop at Cracow, we had spent 5 hours and 43 minutes in the air—a flight that was long enough to give rein to our thoughts, to gain impressions of the countryside and to bring back old memories.

After inspecting and taking over our accommodation, the *Gruppe* went off on leave. Once these wonderful days of leave were over, we re-assembled in July 1943 for briefing on our new role, and instruction on the Me 410, at the bomber destroyer school at Memmingen.'

The change was not without some sad farewells. Because of the smaller crew of the new aircraft, observers and rear-gunners were no longer needed. Duty required that the comradeship and friendship that had grown up in the course of many operations had now to come to a sudden end. Paratroop units, security units, flying schools and many other establishments absorbed these wary old foxes.

Now the bomber pilots had to be turned into fighter pilots for the defence of the homeland. The new Me 410s were fitted with four rocket launchers under their outer wings; in addition they carried two cannon and heavy machine guns, a hefty punch with which to engage the massive formations of American bombers. The rockets were to split up the enemy formations, so that the bombers could be finished off singly. Conversion began.

The first three Me 410s had been issued to the *Geschwader* at Illesheim, in mid-June. As aircraft trickled in, the *Gruppen* were gradually re-equipped and conversion training proceeded; the first confrontation with the bomber formations was not far off. Everyone waited tensely for the day, feeling some apprehension at the prospect of the first encounter. It came on September 6th, 1943.

*I Gruppe*, with 10 or 12 Me 410s fitted with rocket dischargers, took the air against a bomber formation. They met high up over the Black Forest. Two hundred American four-engined bombers, flying close-packed formations, concentrated their defensive fire on their attackers. Even on the run-in, the tracer whistled uncomfortably close; coming in from slightly above and taking evasive action, the *Gruppe* engaged the second wave of the formation at 16,500 feet. The rockets were fired, and streaked away in front of the aircraft on shallow-curved trajectories. A ball of fire in the American formation marked the first success; a bomber turned on its side, and plunged downwards in flames. The nearby bombers were shaken by the blast wave, but flew on. Now the Me 410s were right in the thick of the stream of bombers, and the latter let fly with everything they had.

Captain Winkel had an engine shot out. He dived and broke off, and ordered emergency jettisoning—first of the fuel from the reserve tank, then the ammunition. In this way he was able to hold height and, with the last remaining fuel, he managed to make base at Illesheim for a landing on one engine.

All crews came to the same conclusion after the attack. The success rate was lamentable. Bombers shot down were matched by the defenders own losses, and after the first mission the *Gruppe* was no longer operational. The unit was reinforced; new crews came in and, very slowly, new aircraft.

Before the end of September the unit was transferred to Hoersching. On October 2nd they took off for another operation, and assembled over Zeltweg in the Alps at 28,000 feet. But unfortunately the bombers flying in over Italy turned away and the fighter crews, who had been keyed up for battle, had to land back at Hoersching without having made contact.

Obviously these operations, and the contrast between losses and the expected successer, had given the High Command quite a headache. So the Reichsmarschall in person came down to read the riot act to the commanders. Many a tale was told of the reprimands Hermann Goering used to hand out and of his pet phrases—'Cowardice in the face of the enemy'—and all the biting comments that carried little conviction. For many units the outcome was relief from the sphere of activity and a 'punishment posting' for operations against England. But you can't make fighter-pilots out of bomber crews in a day.

The rocket warheads had a habit, after a long approach flight at high altitude, of failing to detonate at the target; the fuzes had simply frozen.

The Commander-in-Chief of the *Luftwaffe*, Reichsmarschall Hermann Goering, chose Monday, October 11th, for a visit to the fighter units stationed in the area round Fels am Wagram.

Major Klaus Haeberlen, the *I Gruppe* Commander, was ordered to attend with his adjutant, 1st Lieut Werner Pape. Two fighter *Gruppen* were on parade and Haeberlen, as senior officer, reported the parade to the Reichsmarschall. The usual chat about operations and successes sprang up between them.

Asked about problems, Haeberlen, with some feeling, explained how the Me 410 with only single-stage superchargers was no match for the 4-engined American bombers with two-stage supercharging when both were at heights between 12,500 and 20,000 feet. This was not at all to the taste of the Commander-in-Chief and his staff. In the course of the argument which followed, this dashing officer who had proved his worth in many an operation and held the Knight's Cross, was accused by Goering of cowardice in front of the whole parade. On Goering's insistence the Director of Bombers, Colonel Dieter Peltz, had no choice but to relieve Haeberlen of his command.

On October 14th the *Gruppe* was ordered into action once more. The men raced to their machines, and the mass take-off began. One of the rear aircraft was caught in the take-off turbulence, when running at high speed just before lift-off, and broke formation. Its port airscrew sliced through the fuselage of the aircraft next to it about 3 feet in front of the tail. This machine with its tail cut off sat down on its stump, staggered across the field, and came to rest. The machine that had broken formation spun round, and also stopped. For these two crews the operation was over before it had begun. Two aircraft were destroyed, but the crews had survived unhurt.

The rest were ordered by radio to head west, and steadily gained height. The *Gruppe* flew in open formation to meet the 291 bombers of the 8th USAAF, which had been reported over the Frankfurt area. Near Schweinfurt they at last gained visual contact with the bombers, which had already attacked the ball-bearing factory. The twin-engined fighters pursued the bombers, fired their rockets and followed them in. Once again they found themselves in a curtain of fire, in the middle of a tightly-packed formation of bombers.

Schweinfurt was the unit's last mission in home air defence. On November 6th the *Gruppe* moved to Lagerlechfeld to retrain in instrument and night flying on the Me 410, with a view to operations against England. The machine had not really been designed for this role, but after modifications which included the installation of additional equipment and the removal of the rocket dischargers under the wings, the first night circuits were made. Cross-country night flights and exercises over South Germany followed.

The Me 410's landing speed, much higher than that of the Ju 88, and the various automatic systems for flaps and undercarriage, posed severe problems for the young crews who now joined *KG 51*. For instance, in one week of night flying three aircraft made belly-landings on the concrete runway, after their pilots thought they had put their wheels down.

Every belly-landing represented a serious loss to the aircraft strength, which was not generous at the best of times. And every time there was a board of inquiry to determine whether there was any question of sabotage. Punishment was then dished out for irresponsible conduct and damaging government property. And as a result many a pilot came to spend a week inside the 'glasshouse'. In view of the military situation, punishments like this were laughable. In those days the guardroom at Lagerlechfeld contained more battle-experienced, young pilots than thugs or villains.

On December 6th the first elements of *I Gruppe* moved to Evreux in France for raids on England, using a special, parachute-stabilised 1 ton bomb. The *1st Staffel* was at St André, *2nd Staffel* in Dreux and *3rd Staffel* with the Headquarters at Evreux. Now the unit was faced with a new set of problems.

The British AA-defences and night fighters, with their outstanding target-location systems, did not take long to pick up an aircraft, however high it was flying; and they were just as quick at bringing it under heavy fire. The searchlight batteries frequently held the bombers at the target; then even at 23,000 feet, it was light as day in the cockpit, and there was no need for torches to read the maps. So new defensive tactics had to be worked out, if bomber crews were to have any chance of getting alive out of this witches' brew of advanced technology.

A further extract from Adolf Schwachenwald's diary gives a picture of the routine in those days.

On February 20th, 1944 my pilot, Captain Winkel, and I flew as *1st Staffel* advance party to St André. On February 23rd the weather forecast was favourable for a night operation over England, so we gatecrashed the other *Staffel* and did our first sortie over England, in a mass raid on London. The machines took off in the dark at two-minute intervals; airfield and control lights were switched on for a short time only, and then the dark night swallowed us up. The outward flight followed a zig-zag course which had to be flown with precision at predetermined heights. Over the Channel we received a warm welcome, in the shape of British shipborne *Flak* and a gigantic illuminating rocket. Then came the searchlights, like ghostly fingers reaching into the night sky after us, to be followed shortly afterwards by the heavy gun batteries on the coast, whose salvoes were well on for line but out for height. Things were crashing and bursting all round our ears, and under these conditions it took nerves of steel to hold the laid-down course and arrive at the target at the right time for the flares. The timings of the start of target illumination and the attack were staggered by a few minutes. During this interval our 'man at the top', the pathfinder up at 33,000 feet, kept dropping flares. This was our first operation against England and we arrived over the target rather too early; we made a full circuit over the north of the city, then flew in on the red flare to drop our bombs on the city below us, which was burning at many points. Thus relieved of its load, our aircraft leapt upwards and we began a high-speed gradual descent at 380–440mph towards the Channel and the French coast, still under fire.

Over the Channel tracer from an exchange of fire between ships and MTBs looked like carefully laid-out pearl necklaces.

A few hundred yards from us a German machine was shot down by night-fighters, and plunged into the Channel in flames. We had gooseflesh as we heard their last emergency call on the radio: 'Ju 88, call sign . . . SOS . . . we are on fire and losing height'.

After a few minutes we had dry land below us, and were establishing radio communication for landing. Once again, as at take-off, the airfield lights were flashed on only for a few moments, while aircraft were actually landing. Excited, shivering with tension and bathed in sweat, we heaved a sigh of relief when we felt the ground under our wheels. At 23.28hrs, after 1 hour 58 minutes in the air and a flight the like of which we had never experienced before, we climbed out of our aircraft.

Our assessment—anyone who's going to make more than one trip over England these days needs the devil's own luck, and all the gods on his side too.'

On the next day this crew flew back to Lechfeld to debrief on their first operation over England. Then on February 29th the whole of *1st Staffel* moved up into the accommodation prepared for it at St André, near Evreux. There Captain Unrau, *I Gruppe* Commander, had moved in with his Headquarters shortly after handing over his old *1st Staffel* to 1st Lieut Werner Pape. The newly-promoted Lieut Colonel Wolf-Dietrich Meister was commanding the *Geschwader* at this time.

The weather was bad, so that it was not until March 13th that the trips into the British cauldron began. About ten further raids were made on Brighton, London, Bristol and Portsmouth. Every time two or three crews, good friends, were caught in the web of the British defences.

To conceal their exact position from the British tracking stations, bomber crews spent the whole flight throwing out bundles of tinfoil strips. Quite apart from the *Flak*, the crews needed all their luck and skill to avoid destruction by night-fighters.

The long-range night-fighter *Staffel* of *KG 51*, was formed under Major Dietrich Puttfarken, Knight's Cross. The men in this special *Staffel* had the task of catching the British night-fighters as they were flying back to their bases and shooting them down just before they landed. Puttfarken himself was killed near Cambridge on April 22nd, while engaged in one of these operations.

After having been almost wiped out in these operations, *I Gruppe* was posted home shortly before D-Day. On June 3rd, the *Geschwader* Commander, Colonel Wolf-Dietrich Meister, welcomed his men with the news that they were to convert to the Me 262 jet fighter-bomber.

Meanwhile *II Gruppe* had been going ahead with its conversion to the Me 410, under the aegis of Major Josef Schoelss' *IV Gruppe* at Hildesheim. After their training some of the crews moved to Chartres in France and Gilzer-Rijen in Holland in the long-range night-fighter role, to attack Allied bombers as they returned from raids over Germany; Warrant Officer Baier and Senior Warrant Officer Trenke distinguished themselves by shooting down several 4-engined bombers in this way. Following a 'demarcation dispute' that arose between the Director of Bombers and the Director of Night Fighters, however, *II./KG 51* was pulled out of this role and the conversion programme on the Me 410 was abandoned. Later, in October, the *Gruppe* converted to the Me 262 2a.

On June 30th *I Gruppe* of Fast Bomber *Geschwader* 10, equipped with the Fw 190, came under the command of *KG 51*; designated as its *III Gruppe*, it was to operate in the night close support role. But its existence was short-lived, and at the end of October it was disbanded.

*KG 51* was equipped with the Me 410 for less than nine months, but in this time it lost 138 men—45 officers, 72 senior ranks and 21 airmen.

# *VII Stormy Petrel, the Me 262 Jet*

The history of the 'wonderbird', the Me 262, has been written many times. On Hitler's orders this epoch-making high-performance fighter of the future was forced into service as a bomber—the 'hit-and-run' bomber. The first operational jet-fighter in the world, this Messerschmitt design with its two Jumo 004 jet engines was to demonstrate its superiority in battle and open a new chapter in aviation history—not only for Germany.

Captain Wendel, holder of the world air speed record for piston engine powered flight, had demonstrated its handling qualities to the Director of Fighters, General Adolf Galland, in May 1943. After a flight of his own, Galland observed enthusiastically: 'It was 'just like being pushed by an angel'. It would be difficult to find a description of this new design that was more to the point.

The Me 262 was an aircraft with good flying qualities; but it was necessary to pay close attention both to the checklist and to the results of the maker's trials reports. This machine called for precise handling from its pilot. In the climb the needle of the airspeed indicator quickly reached figures beyond those hitherto attained in the most daring of dives. And on top of this it was so quiet in the cockpit that the pilot could imagine himself in a glider. The broad wing made for safety on take-off and landing, though negligent weight distribution could be fatal.

The Me 262 was initially designed as a fighter. It had two fuel tanks each holding 200 gallons, and four 30mm cannon. When Hitler ordered its use as a bomber, drastic modifications had to be undertaken and these reduced its original performance. In addition to the two main fuel tanks mounted fore and aft of the cockpit, two further tanks were fitted, one of 55 gallons under the pilot's seat and the other of 130 gallons in the fuselage behind the rear main tank, a long way from the aircraft's centre of gravity.

On operations this was balanced by two 550lb bombs, to carry which two of the four cannon had to be dismounted. Without these bombs and with the 130 gallon tank full, the machine was so tail-heavy that it was dangerous to fly. Thus this rear tank was never filled for a flight without a bomb-load, and when flying with bombs it had to be emptied first. Some aircraft probably crashed because in the heat of the battle the pilot handled the fuel-cocks incorrectly. If the forward tank was emptied first by mistake and the bombs then released the aircraft, now tail-heavy, would rear up viciously; the elevators could not restore a horizontal attitude.

In high-speed flight too, limits were laid down for the Me 262. Up to 570 mph the control surfaces operated faultlessly, but between 585 and 630 mph the aircraft became uncontrollable. It is reasonable to suppose that some crashes were caused by flying in excess of the aerodynamic limit speed.

Control of the engines gave rise to far more problems than the aerodynamic qualities, however. Most of the pilots who converted to this new aircraft were very experienced; but gas-turbine engines were new territory for them, and some old dogs had to learn a lot of new tricks and learn them quickly. Mounted in the air intake there was a small two-stroke motor, known as the 'tickler', which ran the turbine up to 2,000rpm from which point it could pick up under its own power. But this 'tickler' was temperamental. It was started electrically or with a toggle-line, but frequently this was achieved only by a lot of coaxing and technical sleight of hand; sometimes it would not start at all. Once the support of the 'tickler' had been enlisted, it was clutched-in to the turbine. Ignition was initiated at 800rpm, and at 2,000rpm the 'tickler' was declutched. Then the turbine could be gradually run up to full revs (8,300rpm).

Starting up, and throttle handling, required skill. Opening the throttle too quickly could cause the compressor to stall, and the engine would cut. Moreover the turbine was made of an alloy which, due to raw material shortages, was not resilient enough for the loads imposed on it; * if there was a fault in the fuel metering system, the turbine was likely to overheat and disintegrate. Many a pilot who had got into the habit of knocking forward the throttle and then easing it back, found himself with engines literally falling to pieces.

In retrospect, it must be said that aerodynamically and structurally the Me 262 was brilliant, and far ahead of its time. A cruising speed of 525mph and an hour's endurance were fantastic achievements for these days. It was a pity that no more reliable engine was available.

The Me 262 conversion programme was carried out at Lechfeld. Experts from the manufacturer, in particular Captain Fritz Wendel in the role of flying and technical adviser, were indefatigable in their effors to instruct the *Luftwaffe* aircrew and technicians on the finer points of the 'wonderbird'. Colonel Meister with the *Geschwader* Headquarters

* By this stage of the war the Germans were desperately short of nickel and chromium, two ingredients necessary for the production of high-temperature-resistant alloys.

moved in there on June 2nd and waited for his entourage, who were busy handing over their Me 410s. Once again *KG 51* had been given the distinction to be one of the first *Luftwaffe* formations with the latest equipment.

Unlike the Ju 88, the Me 262 was not fitted with a downward-looking bomb sight; it simply had a reflector sight designed for firing cannon. Nevertheless, given practice, pilots were able to achieve a reasonable bombing accuracy with this device.

Right up to the end of the war, the enemy AA gunner never quite got the measure of the Me 262's speed. As their tracer showed, most of the rounds were well behind an attacking machine.

Enemy fighters on the other hand, especially the Tempests, were able to close the Me 262 by diving from above; and this was easier still if the jet aircraft was laden with bombs. But the best chance for enemy fighters was to catch the Me 262 as it took off or when it was coming into land with only a few minutes' fuel left. Here the enemy air superiority in the last months of the war really made itself felt.

Until several tragic losses had served to make the point, the aircraft had no armour behind the pilot's head. This was added only in March 1945.

In November and December 1944 KG 51 was taken by surprise by the appearance of severe symptoms of poisoning in pilots who had been shot up and had received burns. For instance Senior Warrant Officer Kohler, who is buried at Bremen, died from this poisoning after being only slightly burnt on the hands. The cause was the fuel used for the gas-turbines. Once this was established, all pilots were issued with expensive leather clothing and thick leather gloves.

After a short period of technical instruction, a start was made with training flights. There was no two-seat version of the Me 262. The instructor gave a pre take-off briefing, supervised the crucial starting-up procedure, and in case of need gave the pilot radio instructions on how to handle the aircraft. Everyone was astonished at how well the pilots performed.

Meanwhile, with the Allied landings on the north coast of France between Cherbourg and Caen on June 6th, 1944, the expected invasion had begun. But the hit-and-run bombers were not quite operational.

Elements of 3rd *Staffel* were placed under Major Wolfgang Schenck, holder of the Oak Leaves to the Knight's Cross and an officer of considerable dash and determination, to form Special Detachment Schenck (also known as Special Detachment *E 51*). They were to move forthwith to the invasion front to support the ground forces.

Lechfeld soon became a thorn in the Allies' flesh. Their efficient Intelligent network had told them that a new weapon was being tested there, and that it was still in the trials stage. One raid on the airfield destroyed and damaged 60 Me 262s belonging to the Trials Detachment of *KG 51*.

The early aircraft carried no tactical markings on their fuselage but simply bore large, easily visible, letters from A to Z. Various problems arose while the aircraft were being modified for the bomber role at Schwaebisch Hall. Undercarriages and tyres were strengthened and supplementary fuel tanks fitted. There were no proven bomb-racks or bomb-sights. Accurate dive-bombing was impossible; a personal order by Hitler (sic) forbade dives and flying below 13,000 feet over enemy territory, to reduce the chance of an aircraft being hit by AA fire and falling into enemy hands. This condemned the *Geschwader* to failure before it started; the inaccurate bombing was both inevitable and depressing—and it did little for morale when the term 'crop damage *Geschwader*' crept into local conversations. Many of the machines that were flown to Schwaebisch Hall for modification were destroyed by Allied bombing. The 'stormy petrels' were hunted down wherever they might be.

Instruction began on June 20th, a fortnight after the Allies landed in France. By July 20th about twelve pilots from 3 *Staffel* had made just four flights with the new machine and were beginning to get to know it. With the way things were going at the front, this meant that they were now 'operational'. On July 20th, they moved to Châteaudun with nine aircraft, for immediate operations. But even before then the retreat was on, and the evacuation of France began. Enemy pressure on lightly held sectors was irresistible, and on August 12th the Detachment had to move to Etampes.

The groundstaff worked wonders. Since the Me 262's Jumo engines had an average life of only eight hours, there was always somewhere in France a convoy, camouflaged and heavily guarded, laden with engines and spares, weighed down too with every kind of special authority and certificates, looking for Special Detachment *E 51*. The battle-experienced radio operators of Ju 88 and Me 410 days, always managed to find a way of getting to their destination—their unit. On August 15th there came another move, this time to Creil. Then things got too hot for them there too, and on August 22nd the Detachment shifted to Juvincourt near Reims. One of the engine convoys heard about this too late, when still on the way to Creil, and fell intact into Allied hands.

On August 23rd further elements of 3rd *Staffel* were sent to reinforce Detachment Schenck. However, of nine aircraft only five got there. Two crashed on take-off due to incorrect take-off procedure, the third crashed on taking off from the intermediate stop at Schwaebisch Hall, and the fourth could not find Juvincourt and made a good forced landing. From Juvincourt the little Detachment was in action every day against targets on the Seine, northwest of Paris and in the Melun area.

Then the enemy broke through at Soissons, Châlons-sur-Marne, and Vitry-la-François and street-fighting flared up in the town of Juvincourt nearby. On August 28th the Detachment was ordered to move to Ath-Chièvres in Belgium. Over Haltert, near Brussels, Warrant Officer 'Ronny' Lauer was chased by four Spitfires and had to make a forced landing. Luckily the Me 262 belly-landed very well, and did not catch fire before he had made his escape.*

The unit spent its whole time trying to escape enemy fighters and bombers. They stayed at Chièvres only two days and then, on August 30th, they were off to new stations in Holland: Volkel and Eindhoven. They had got used to being chased from pillar to post and were able to fly sorties against targets near Louvain and Antwerp and on the Albert Canal Line. Then, when Volkel was raided in broad daylight by Lancaster and Halifax bombers, the Detachment had to do another move on September 4th back behind the German frontier. At two o'clock in the morning all the survivors crossed the Rhein near Wesel.

*I Gruppe*, into which the Schenck Detachment was now merged, was finding its feet at Rheine-Bentlage, Hoerstel, Dreierwalde and Hopsten. Gradually the *Gruppe* was brought up to strength by machines flown in from Lechfeld. And at last their fuselages bore the familiar tactical marking '9K+' again, and the Edelweiss glittered below the cockpit. Lieut. Colonel Schenck took over command of the entire *Geschwader*. Meanwhile *II Gruppe* under Major Grundmann, preparing at Schwaebisch Hall, had reached a point where they could move to Hesepe near Achmer and go into action in the high-speed bomber role.

Ever since the autumn of 1944 Hitler had been mulling over a great, new and hopefully decisive offensive in the West. Again and again the date for it slipped. Then at 05.30hrs. on December 16th, 1944 there began Operation 'Watch on the Rhine', which was to go down in military history as the Ardennes Offensive.

At first bad weather prevented air operations, but on December 22nd it cleared. Bitter fighting flared up at Bastogne and west of Rochefort. Allied air superiority was crushing. By contrast, the few German bombers could not get through to their targets and suffered heavy losses. Targets had to be engaged from tree-top height—the only way of getting through the enemy fighters. The Me 262's high speed was often the only thing that saved it from the Tempests, which were always lurking over the Hopsten/Achmer and Rheine areas, waiting to shoot down the hit-and-run bombers as they came back to base, just when they were most

* In fact the 'Spitfires' were USAAF Thunderbolts. Major J. Myers and Lt M. Croy of the 82 Fighter Squadron, 78th FG, were credited with the destruction of Lauer's aircraft, the first Me 262 to be destroyed in combat.

vulnerable.

The German airfields were surrounded by AA guns—for example as many as 160 quadruple 20mm cannon on the east-west runway at Rheine. This significantly reduced the Allies' chances of shooting down the Me 262s; in addition piston-engined fighter units always flew close cover for the jet-bomber formations. The Allies were quick to adjust their offensive tactics to this situation.

The Ardennes Offensive soon bogged down; fuel and ammunition were short, and not even the spirit and courage of the German soldier could make up for that. There was not long to wait for the Allied advance into Germany. The *Geschwader* was continuously engaged at the numerous centres of effort. *IV Gruppe* at Munich-Riem and Erding trained volunteer pilots from all the jet bomber *Geschwader*. But many of the old, experienced Ju 88 or Me 410 pilots could not get the feel of the new machine. They had no confidence in the new engines with their 'scream'. The perpetual fuel shortage impeded training. Some 65 tons were needed to train one replacement pilot. Like the aircraft factories, the German synthetic fuel plants were being regularly bombed by the Allies. The raw-material bottlenecks too were steadily becoming more critical.

*II Gruppe* was operating—though with no great success—from Hesepe and Achmer with *Kampfgerschwader 76* which was flying the Arado 234 'Lightning' twin-jet bomber.

During the carpet-bombing raid on Rheine on November 13th many members of *KG 51* were killed, and many others injured. Among the aircrew 1st Lieut Merlau and Warrant Officer Hoffman were killed, and the *I Gruppe* medical officer, Dr. Denkhaus, was among those badly wounded.

At Hesepe too, bombs caused many casualties among the men of 5th *Staffel*. The men of the jet units were marked men, always on the run and hunted down wherever they went. The *Gruppe* Headquarters was forced to move to near Hopsten, whence it rotated between Hoerstel, Dreierwalde and Esch.

The bulk of operations was against targets in the Liège, Antwerp, Nijmwegen, Volkel and Eindhoven areas and troop concentrations resulting from the costly airborne assault at Arnhem. *II Gruppe* was flying from the Essen-Muehlheim field, with its relatively short runway, mainly against enemy positions round Euskirchen, Dueren and Juelich, where bitter fighting was in progress for the Reichswald and the Huertgen-Wald. The Me 262 needed the assistance of rockets to get off this field.

On New Year's Eve 1944 lights out at 19.00hrs was ordered for all *Luftwaffe* units. Something special, with very tight security, was in the air. Even the unit commanders did not know the targets. No one could sleep properly. It was the same in *I Gruppe*, where the technical officer of 3rd *Staffel* at Rheine, Lieut Moser, was down in the hangars with his men far into the night trying to get the highest possible serviceability; but despite this, only 21 machines out of 30 were reported serviceable. Reveille was three o'clock in the morning; the commanding officers and *Staffel* leaders were in the briefing room with sealed envelopes for the crews—target folders for a large-scale low-level attack on allied airfields in Belgium and Holland.

Every pilot received a carefully-prepared map, with strongpoints, airfields and AA-concentrations behind the Allied lines marked on it; even the flight plans for the homeward flight had already been worked out. Take-off was at 07.45hrs. The units were led to the front line by Ju 88 pathfinders—one mass formation made towards Brussels, the second headed for Arnhem and Eindhoven and the third directed on Venlo. The targets for *I./KG 51* on this cold winter morning were the airfields at Eindhoven and 's Hertogenbosch in Holland. As the sun came up the Americans and British were still asleep—no doubt with their heads reeling from New Year's Eve parties. Who would have imagined that the *Luftwaffe* could strike a blow like this—the air force that everyone thought was on its last legs? The airfields lay peacefully below, packed with aircraft of every type.

Soon aircraft, fuel dumps, workshops and administrative buildings were in flames. The surprise attack had succeeded and pillars of black smoke signalled its success.

The raider flew back in a mounting inferno of flak. Dogfights developed and red glows in the snow marked the crashes. The damage to enemy material was massive—810 aircraft destroyed, with 800 German aircraft taking part in the operation. A total of 293 German aircraft were lost, 59 of them with experienced formation leaders—an irreplaceable blood-letting among the key commanders. Enemy AA fire accounted for 200 of these. They had flown along a '*Flak* path' that the Allies had set up against the V1 flying bombs. Among these casualties was one of the oldest and most experienced pilots in the *Geschwader*, Senior Warrant Officer Erich Kaiser. But the severe weakening of the Allied air forces lasted no more than a week. On the same afternoon, January 1st, 1945 the air-mobile elements of the *Gruppe* moved to Giebelstadt; Frankfurt-Rhine/Main was also prepared for the reception of aircraft. But the tempo of the tactical battle was such that nothing really came of this move, and by the end of February they were back in Hopsten. The British were holding along the Rhine north of Kalkar, while the Americans had already begun their onslaught on the Ruhr. When the Americans managed, on March 7th, to seize the slightly damaged Rhine bridge at Remagen and form a bridgehead, the duty officer of *I./KG 51* at Hopsten received a personal call from Reichsmarschall Goering, ordering the unit to call forthwith for volunteers to dive onto the Remagen bridge, just as if they were Japanese Kamikaze pilots. Two men came forward, but the mission was never flown. It was too late.

On March 13th the first crews moved down to Leipheim, where one took off on the autobahn and landed on the airfield runway, taxiing straight under the trees to seek cover and concealment. For an operations room these jet-bomber crews used the Leipheim/Guenzburg autobahn café.

Other elements of the *Gruppe* were at Giebelstadt. The focal point of operations was in Lower Alsace in the Hagenau Forest area. It was here that Lieut Ritter von Rittersheim was killed in action at Rittershofen; and in the course of one of these missions Lieut Batel shot down an American Thunderbolt over Karlsruhe—the bomber men could do that too when the need arose.

In Leipheim a tragic incident occurred. Thanks to the steadily mounting chaos that prevailed in the *Luftwaffe* the *Geschwader* had two commanders at once. Major Barth had an official letter appointing him to the command, and Lieut Colonel von Halensleben had another one. As von Halensleben was driving in his staff car over the Leipheim autobahn bridge, he was shot up by American fighter-bombers, and he and three other men were killed. They were buried at Leipheim.

From then on Barth was to command the *Geschwader* to the bitter end. From Leipheim targets were attacked in the Wuerzburg, Tauberbischofsheim and Crailsheim areas—in fact all over the Swabian and Franconian provinces. Meanwhile II *Gruppe*, operating from Schwaebisch Hall, was committed on the Rhine near Speyer and round Kaiserslautern. On March 21st the popular leader of *3 Staffel*, Captain Winkel, who had so often proved his worth and had just taken off on his 300th operational sortie, was killed on the edge of the field at Giebelstadt by a stray bullet from an American Thunderbolt. He was hit in the head, and as a result of this all Me 262s were immediately fitted with a thick armour plate in the cockpit behind the pilot's neck.

It was not long before the thunder of Allied artillery was ringing once again in everyone's ears. All the jet fighter bases were being continuously hammered by Allied bombs, and the end was not far off. On April 21st *I Gruppe* went to Memmingen, and *II Gruppe* pulled back via Nuernberg-Fuerth to Linz/Hoersching. The Americans were in front of Ulm and Munich. The signs of a once so well-knit army breaking up were hard to live with. Everywhere the 'hero's pitchfork' went round gathering local defence units. Even with plenty of luck and a special pass saying '. . . is a member of a jet unit and by Hitler's orders must not be employed on ground defence duties', aircrew had the greatest difficulty in escaping the Volksturm's net.

About 80% of *II Gruppe* under Major Grundmann were captured by the Americans at Strasskirchen, near Landau/Isar. The rest of the *Staffel* got to Kammern near Landau under 1st Lieut. Baetz.

*I Gruppe* just managed to get clear of Memmingen at the last moment with its aircraft and groundstaff. Some sorties were flown against the Danube bridges at Dillingen as a last gesture of resistance. On the afternoon of April 23rd the cry 'French closing on Memmingen' echoed round the Memmingen airfield; the crews bounded out of the mess and flew their aircraft to Munich-Riem, where the Me 262s were handed over to General Galland's fighter force. As soon as they landed the machines were towed well away from the field for concealment; an air-raid alarm soon chased up any stragglers.

The digging of foxholes in the stony ground of Riem caused the airmen much sweat and tears; they were not used to physical labour. Quite often two airmen would jump in the same foxhole as the bombs burst all round them, and then wonder why there wasn't enough room. While most of *I Gruppe* pulled out to the Schoenegg-Nordhof estate at Dietramszell (near Holzkirchen), a few had to stay behind for a special task. At the end of April, and with a heavy heart Dr Woernle, *IV Gruppe* technical officer, had to blow up about fifty Me 262s at Neuberg/Donau when the airfield came under American artillery fire.

As dawn broke on April 30th, 1945, Munich too came under American artillery fire. A rising broke out in Czechoslovakia, and the turncoat Russian General Vlassov's troops, up till then German allies, joined it. The German Armed Forces intervened, to cover the retreat of their own troops and the evacuation of German refugees.

Seven dutiful volunteers under Captain Abrahamczik took back their trusty machines and flew via Hoersching to Prague-Rusin. A small team of brave mechanics followed them by road to look after the aircraft; they took a few workshop vehicles with them, but were faced with every kind of difficulty and had to improvise as they went along. In Prague this small group was put under command of 'Hogeback Force'. They took part in the fighting in and around Prague and had to learn the difficult task of supporting street and house-to-house fighting from the air. Lieut Schimmel was killed in action on May 6th, and 1st Lieut Strothmann and Sergeant Poling on the following day.

The situation was becoming more and more difficult. Prague-Russin was evacuated on May 6th, and the detachment moved to Zatec. Here there was nothing left with which to fight, and they set about defending themselves as best they could. There was no fuel or spares, and the groundstaff had not joined them. They gave themselves up to the

Americans in Prague, Zatec or Pilsen, to avoid being taken prisoner by the Russians or the Czechs. Some of them were later handed over to the Russians, and were never seen again.

On May 8th, after the signature of a surrender on the British front had been announced, Captain Abrahamczik briefed the pilots who were still with him only to land in areas held by troops from the West. Early on May 7th the overall surrender of the German Armed Forces was completed at Rheims, and 00.01hrs., May 9th, became the official date for the ending of hostilities.

Everyone's future suddenly went blank; their world had collapsed around them. Their only thought now was to survive. The four remaining pilots of the detachment considered how to make the best of this hopeless situation. The last flight, in a previously full life of flying and soldiering, stood before them. These men had always found their way out of a tight corner before; and the clear blue sky left little room for low spirits. Despite everything they felt a certain confidence. However bad things were, life had to go on—only not in the East; they knew all about that already.

The question that confronted a German soldier on May 8th, 1945, the day of the surrender, was not 'What shall I do?' but 'Where shall I go?'. For Lieut Wilhelm Batel there was only one answer: 'Home if I can; and if I can't, to an airfield in British hands.' This is the story of his flight.

He took off from Zatec at 14.30hrs on May 8th in 9K + FB and headed straight for Lueneburg. It was wonderful weather with excellent visibility. He flew at about 10,000feet. He remembers his flight to this day, and not without reason. Overnight things had changed in a way that he could not at the time envisage. The dangers of war were past. His aircraft was fully armed, but to what end? The scene was completely unfamiliar—no flak, no fires from air-raids, no steaming railway engines; on the airfields at Dresden, Leipzig (he had learnt instrument flying at Machern) and Magdeburg the allied machines stood drawn up as if on parade. Just after 15.00hrs he reached the Lueneburg airfield, which was obviously in British hands. His parents lived on a farm about 20 miles away. His intention of buzzing them to show he was alive was frustrated by navigation problems: he had learnt the country round his home mainly on foot and not in a cockpit. His Me 262 spoilt his feel for the ground. But he soon managed to adjust to this.

As he flew over the small estate he saw that in the village and on the main roads round it there was heavy military traffic—jeeps and trucks. To land right by it would be stupid. With this in mind he spotted a field about 2 miles away on the edge of a wood; there were no troops or people around. At 15.28hrs he swept in for his last landing. He made a perfect belly-landing in the field of wheat and his aircraft came to rest about 10 yards from the edge of the wood. With his briefcase and his parachute he quickly got under cover.

He then started to walk towards his home; but quite near where he had landed, as he was crossing a ride, he met a farmhand who did not recognise him. So he asked him the way to somewhere on the other side of the spot where he had landed. This turned out to be a good thing, for later the British embarked on a very intensive search and the information the man passed on kept him clear of this. About 16.30hrs he reached Weissen Berg which gave him a view over his parents' village, but not the part where they lived. So he lay down in the sun and watched what was going on in the village and the roads round it. When it started to get dark, using trees, hedges and fences for cover, he made his way across the half-mile or so of open country to the other end of the village and reached his parents' house without being spotted. The barking of his parents' Alsatians announced his presence.

The reunion was a happy one but very subdued, for there were a lot of refugees living in the house. After a few days Wilhelm Batel came out of hiding and gave out that he had been officially discharged.

The flight leader, Captain Abrahamczik escorted 1st Lieut. Haeffner, who could not get his undercarriage up because of a technical fault. They flew to Munich-Riem, from where they had set off for their adventurous operations in Czechoslovakia. The Americans were delighted to take over the two jets, and the pilots went into captivity.

The fourth of this little band, 1st Lieut. Froehlich, chose Fassberg as his destination. He too landed without being spotted. The British there didn't seem in the least put out by this unexpected arrival. They were much too busy celebrating the armistice with the aid of liquid refreshment and songs, and happily gathered this nonplussed German into their midst. It was two days before their heads cleared sufficiently for someone to suggest that this 'enemy airman' ought to have his pistol taken away and be handed over to the Army. So he too did not escape the fate of so many German soldiers—captivity.

The war was over. Germany was beaten. For Germans the flying was over—probably for good.

During the *KG 51's* relatively short spell with the Me 262, 172 of its men had been killed—53 officers, 91 senior ranks and 28 airmen.

Appendix A

# *Note on the Award of Decorations to German Airmen*

The Knight's Cross of the Iron Cross was the most highly-prized military decoration in the German armed forces of the Second World War. This award, introduced on September 1st, 1939 for 'outstanding bravery in the face of the enemy', was an extension of the Order of the Iron Cross, instituted on March 10th, 1813. During the war three further grades were added, these being Oak leaves, Swords and Diamonds.

Out of a total of 7,500 awards of the Knight's Cross, about 1,730 were made to the *Luftwaffe*, of which some 1,320 (including the higher grades) went to aircrew of all ranks. Of these, 538 were conferred on day and night fighter and pursuit fighter personnel, and 640 went to bomber, dive-bomber and ground-attack crews.

The conditions governing awards varied as the war sent on, being based mainly on the number of operational missions. Thus in March 1943, for instance, the standards were as follows:

| *Operational Missions* | *Award* |
|---|---|
| 15 | Iron Cross Class II |
| 20 | Bronze clasp (for operations) |
| 25–40 | Iron Cross Class I |
| 60 | Silver clasp |
| 80 | Trophy of Honour |
| 110 | Gold clasp |
| 140 | German Cross in Gold |
| 200–400 | Knight's Cross of the Iron Cross |

Looking at the bomber awards, one finds that in 1940 they went almost entirely to commanders of *Geschwardern* and *Gruppen*, who were decorated for the most part to mark the contribution their formations had made to the various campaigns. (The first such award went to Colonel Robert Fuchs, KG 26) For other pilots the number of missions lay around 100 by day or night, with emphasis on flights over England.

During 1941 the 'critical number' rose to 200, and in the later years of the war it remained at 200–400, with most receiving the Knight's Cross after some 300 missions. It was noteworthy that crews operating against Russia usually had this number of missions, and often many more, to their credit at the time of an award. Observers, radio operators, flight engineers and gunners had almost always completed well over 300 missions before being decorated and were often members of the crews of particularly successful pilots or formation commanders who themselves already held the Knight's Cross.

The higher grades of the Knight's Cross (4 awards of Swords and 27 of Oakleaves) were awarded only to pilots of exceptional distinction, most of them also *Staffel* leaders or *Gruppe* or *Geschwarder* commanders, who had themselves survived numerous operational missions or who had achieved outstanding successes with their commands.

The Knight's Cross could be conferred posthumously, and awards of it took place even after the official ending of the war.

Appendix B

# *Kampfgeschwader 51 (Edelweiss) Stations (From April 1st, 1937 onwards)*

| *Headquarters* | *I Gruppe* | *II Gruppe* | *III Gruppe* | *IV Gruppe* |
|---|---|---|---|---|
| Landsberg/Lech<br>(1/4/37–20/6/40) | Landsberg<br>(1/4/37–20/8/39) | disbanded (to form 77 Wing)<br>Munich-Riem<br>(1/4–14/6/40) | Memmingen<br>(1/4/37–6/11/39) | |
| | Memmingen<br>(20/8/39–6/5/40)<br>Lechfeld<br>(6/5–20/6/40) | | Landsberg<br>6/11/39–20/6/40) | |
| | | Stuttgart-Echterdingen<br>(14/6–18/6/40) | | |
| Paris–Orly<br>(20/6/40–30/3/41) | Paris–Orly<br>(20/6-1/8/40)<br>Villaroche<br>(1/8/40–30/3/41) | Etampes–Mondésir<br>(20/6–24/8/40)<br>Paris–Orly<br>24/8/40–12/4/41) | Etampes–Mondésir<br>(20/6–3/11/40)<br>Brétigny<br>(3/11/40–30/3/41) | Lechfeld<br>(10/1–22/4/41) |
| Wiener–Neustadt<br>(30/3–16/4/41) | Wiener–Neustadt<br>(20/3–16/4/41)<br>Krumovo<br>(16/4–14/5/41)<br>Wiener–Neustadt<br>(14/5–4/6/41) | Wiener–Neustadt<br>(12/4–20/6/41) | Wiener–Neustadt<br>(30/3–18/6/41) | Wiener–Neustadt<br>(22/4–24/12/41) |

| *Headquarters* | *I Gruppe* | *II Gruppe* | *III Gruppe* | *IV Gruppe* |
|---|---|---|---|---|
| Krosno (4/6–15/7/41) | Krosno (4/6–4/7/41) Luck (4–15/7/41) | Krosno (20–27/6/41) Balti (27/6–8/9/41) | Lezany (18/6–5/7/41) Vlodzimierrs (5–18/7/41) Wiener–Neustadt (Refresher training to 30/8/41) | Wiener–Neustadt |
| Zilistea/Balti (15/7–17/10/41) | Zilistea (15/7–10/10/41) | Wiener–Neustadt (Refresher training to 4/12/41) | Balti (30/8–23/10/41) | Wiener–Neustadt |
| Nikolayev (17/10/41–3/4/42) | Tiraspol (10/10/41–24/1/42) Refresher training (Odessa) to 3/4/42 | Nikolayev, Kitay (4–12/12/41) | Nikolayev (23/10/41–24/3/42) Refresher training (Odessa) to 15/5/42 | Wiener–Neustadt |
| Zaporoshye (3/4–10/7/42) | Zaporoshye (3/4–30/5/42) Charkov–W (30/5–10/7/42) | Zaporoshye (12/12/41–7/9/42) Charkov–W (29/5–10/7/42) | Zaporoshye (15–29/5/42) | Bobruysk (24/12/41–11/8/43) |
| Stalino (10/7–12/9/42) | Stalino (10/7–5/8/42) Kertsh (5–19/8/42) Tatsinskaya (19/8–23/9/42) | Stalino (7/9–20/9/42) | Stalino (10/7–5/8/42) Kertsh (5–20/8/42) Tatsinskaya (20/8–28/9/42) | Bobruysk |
| Bagerovo (12/9–8/10/42) | Tatsinskaya | Bagerovo (20/9–25/10/42) | Tatsinskaya | Bobruysk |

| | | | | |
|---|---|---|---|---|
| Sarabus<br>(8/10–7/12/42) | Sarabus<br>(6/10–3/11/42)<br>Tatsinskaya<br>(3/11–7/12/42) | Armavir<br>(25/10–6/11/42)<br>(no aircraft) | Sarabus<br>(28/9–20/12/41) | Bobruysk |
| Rostov<br>(7/12/42–5/2/43) | Rostov<br>(7/12/42–5/2/43) | Bagerovo<br>(no aircraft) | Rostov<br>(20/12/42–6/2/43) | Bobruysk |
| Zaporoshye<br>(5/2–27/2/43) | Zaporoshye<br>(5/2–2/4/43) | Zaporoshye<br>(6/2–8/5/43) | Zaporoshye<br>(6–27/2/43) | Bobruysk |
| Bagerovo<br>(27/2–8/5/43) | Bagerovo<br>(2/4–8/5/43) | Bryansk<br>(8/5–26/7/43) | Bagerovo<br>(27/2–10/5/43) | Bobruysk |
| Bryansk<br>(8/5–26/7/43) | Illesheim<br>(8/5–6/8/43) | Bryansk | Bryansk<br>(10/5–21/7/43) | Bobruysk |
| Seshchinskaya<br>(26/7–16/8/43) | Memmingen/Lechfeld<br>(6/8–30/8/43) | Seshchinskaya<br>(26/7–1/8/43) | Seshchinskaya<br>(21/7–9/8/43) | Hildesheim<br>(11/8/43–1/4/44) |
| Kirovograd<br>(16/8–7/9/43) | Illesheim<br>(30/8–29/9/43) | Kirovograd, Charkov,<br>Shitomir<br>(1/9–18/9/43) | Kirovograd<br>(9/8–31/8/43) | Hildesheim |
| Illesheim<br>(7/9–6/12/43) | Hoersching<br>(29/9–6/12/43) | Saloniki<br>(18/9–6/12/43) | Illesheim<br>(31/8–31/12/43) | Hildesheim |
| Evreux<br>(6/12/43–15/2/44) | Evreux<br>(6/12/43–25/4/44) | Kalinovka<br>(28/11/43–4/1/44)<br>Vinniza<br>(4/1–8/1/44)<br>Lublin<br>(8/1–Apr. 44) | (disbanded 31/12/43) | Munich–Riem<br>(1/4–29/12/44)<br>redesignated<br>IV Squadron,<br>1 Wing, and also<br>stationed at<br>Neuburg and<br>Erding. |

| *Headquarters* | *I Gruppe* | *II Gruppe* | *III Gruppe* | *IV Gruppe* |
|---|---|---|---|---|
| St. Georges–Môtel (15/2–23/5/44) Lechfeld (23/5–5/9/44) | Dreux/St. André (25/4–23/5/44) Lechfeld/Leipheim (23/5–20/7/44) | Gilze–Riyen (Apr.–Aug. 44) Schwaebisch Hall (Aug.–Sept. 44) | I Squadron, 10 Wing, redesignated III Squadron, 51 Wing and subsequently disbanded. | |
| | Chateaudun (20/7–12/8/44) Etampes (12–15/8/44) | Schwaebisch Hall | | Munich–Riem |
| | Creil (15–27/8/44) Corbeny Juvincourt (27–28/8/44) Ath–Chievres (28–30/8/44) Volkel (30/8–5/9/44) | Achmer/Hesepe | | |
| Rheine/Hoerstel/ Hopsten (5/9/44–20/3/45) | Rheine/Hoerstel/ Hopsten (5/9/44–20/3/45) | Essen–Muelheim | | |
| Giebelstadt | Giebelstadt | Schwaebisch Hall | (disbanded) | Munich–Riem |

| (20–30/3/45) | 20–30/3/45) | Fuerth<br>Linz/Hoersching | 30/3/45 Aircraft<br>handed over to<br>No 44 Fighter Unit |
|---|---|---|---|
| Leipheim<br>(30/3–21/4/45)<br>Memmingen<br>(21–24/4/45)<br>Holzkirchen<br>(21–30/4/45)<br>Then attached to<br>Motorised Detachment<br>103, Air Force<br>Ground Defence | Leipheim<br>(30/3–21/4/45)<br>Memmingen<br>(21–24/4/45)<br>Munich–Riem<br>(21–30/4/45) | Landau/Isar<br>disbanded<br>on 24/5/45 and<br>placed under command<br>of an infantry<br>brigade as ground<br>troops | |
| | Prague–Rusin<br>(30/4–6/5/45)<br>Zatec<br>(6/5–8/5/45)<br>Detachment disbanded<br>Some personnel<br>were attached to Air<br>Force Ground<br>Defence Detachment<br>and Air Force<br>"Security Group"<br>in the Alpine Redoubt | | |

Appendix C

# *Organisation of a Bomber Geschwader*

In war the daily round of operations drives everything else into the background. Few aircrew had time or opportunity to worry about *Geschwader* organisation. Anyone who has ever served on a military staff will be familiar with the terms 'establishment' and 'war-establishment'. These documents gave, for a headquarters, a *Gruppe*, a *Staffel* or any other unit, the organisation, the specialisations and strengths of officers, NCOs, rank and file and attached civilians, and also the scale of equipment and armament. But the exigencies of war all too often meant that the reality bore little resemblance to the planned war-establishment.

A bomber *Geschwader* was made up of three first-line *Gruppen* and a further *Gruppe*, (*IV Gruppe*) for reinforcement training. Each *Gruppe* had attached to it an Airfield-support company and a Headquarters Company.

A *Gruppe* was subdivided into three operational *Staffeln*, each consisting of nine to twelve aircraft with their aircrew, technical groundstaff and general duties men. With the reconnaissance *Staffeln* included, the maximum aircraft strength was 200; of these 110 to 120 on an average would be serviceable and available for operations, the rest being under scheduled maintenance or repair. In terms of personnel a bomber *Geschwader* was around 2,500 strong.

The notes below will explain some of the Roman numerals, abbreviations and functions mentioned in the tables which follow. (In the absence of full documentation the tables make no claim to being comprehensive.)

| | |
|---|---|
| Staff Major (administration) | An officer not on flying duties and responsible for routine matters ('the static pole'). |
| Ia | Operations |
| Io | Battle and technical intelligence (e.g. enemy aircraft types, armaments, strengths, etc.)—but no cloak and dagger stuff. |
| IIa | Personnel—officers |

| | |
|---|---|
| IIb | Personnel—airmen (Adjutant) |
| I N/NVW | Navigation and communications staff |
| I TO | Technical officers (aircrew) |
| IVa | Attached civilian in the administrative section (Welfare, administration, canteen services) |
| IVb | Medical officer (aircrew and groundstaff) |
| Ln 0 | Radio officer (Telecommunications) |

## Organisation of a Bomber Geschwader

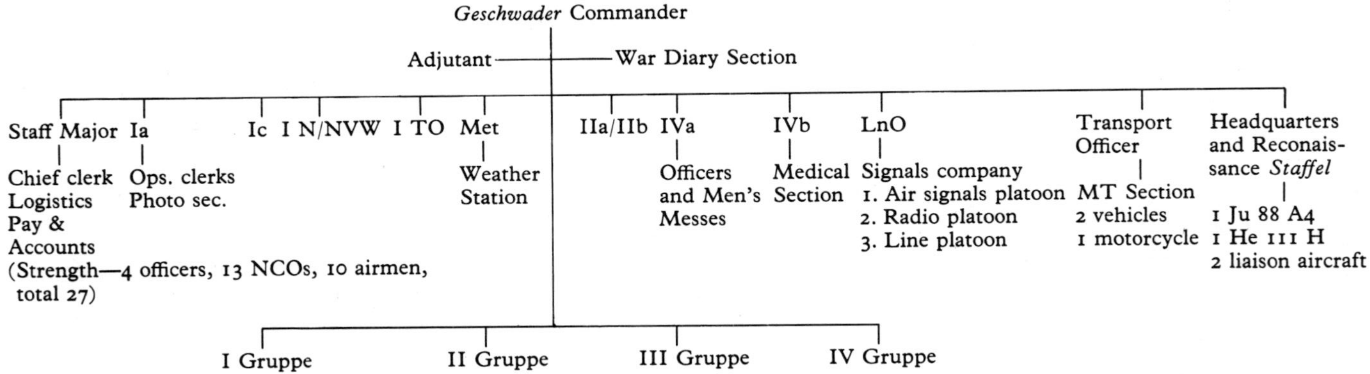


## Organisation of a Gruppe

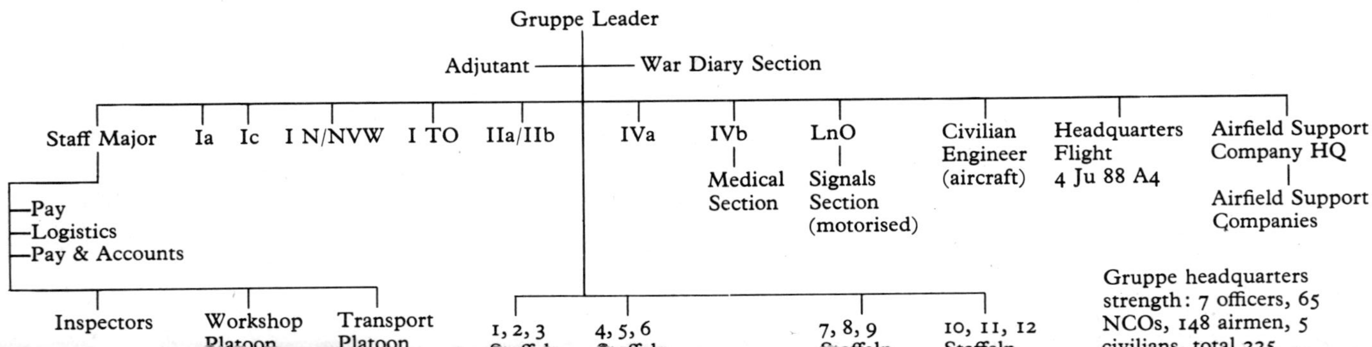

- Radio — Armaments
- Parachutes (Rescue & safety equipment). — Technical Stores

## Organisation of a Staffel

*Staffel* Leader

- Warrant Officer
- Administrative officer

- Flight headquarters
  - War diary section
  - Pay & Accounts
  - Transport

  9 vehicles
  1 motorcycle

- TO Groundstaff
  - Airframe fitters
  - Instrument mechanics
  - Radio mechanics
  - Technical stores
  - Engine fitters
  - Electricians
  - Armourers
  - Parachutes (Rescue and safety equipment)
  - Refuelling

  12 Ju 88 A4

- Signals Section
- Mess

*Flight strength:* 14 officers 67 NCOs, 50 airmen. Total 131.

Appendix D

# *The Airfield Support Company*

The Airfield Support Company's primary task was to ensure that the first-line *Gruppen* and *Staffeln* were operational and got airborne. These companies were formed at the beginning of 1938 from men of the old (static) airfield and headquarters companies and specialists from the first-line *Staffeln,* to bring all the technical specialists into one formed body and so to make the best possible use of them in the support of flying. *KG 51's* airfield support companies did not confine themselves to 'their' formation, but also gave technical support to fighter and heavy-fighter units. Towards the end of 1943 a redesignation took place by which 1 Airfield Support Company, *KG 51,* became 143 Airfield Support Company and 8 Airfield Support Company, *KG 51* 112 Airfield Support Company. Transfers were the order of the day.

Under its company commander, who was usually an experienced engineer and technical officer, the 150-strong Airfield Support Company had a Company Warrant Officer ('the sergeant major'). Under him came a company headquarters, 8–10 men strong, consisting of clerks, pay clerks, cooks and a quartermaster sergeant.

Each first-line flight was supported by a technical platoon of some 30 men, made up of:

Platoon leader (Chief artificer), 12 airframe fitters, 2 engine fitters, 1 instrument mechanic, 6 armourers (bombs), 6 armourers (weapons), 2 radio mechanics and 1 parachute repairer (rescue and safety equipment).

A workshop platoon of specialists capable of dealing with any light and medium repairs that might arise provided a back-up. This consisted of:

1 platoon leader, 12 engine fitters, 4 sheet-metal workers, 2 painters, 1 harness repairer, 2 carpenters and a few other tradesmen. These men were given their basic military training in air training brigades, and their technical training was carried out in specialised air technical schools. The average age of the members of these companies was between 20 and 25, and all were career airmen.

Appendix E

# *Motorised Air Signals Company, KG 51*

In practice, apart from the radio operators in their crews, bomber *Geschwadern* received signals support from the static communications branches of the airfield headquarters; but right at the beginning of the war the need became clear to provide *Geschwadern* with their own air signals companies. To this end mobile platoons were formed from the static communications organisation in Saxony and South Germany, and these were later brought together as Air Signals Company, *KG 51*. The company was under command of the *Geschwader* commander for all purposes, receiving only specialised technical instructions from the signals staff at higher formation headquarters. In contrast to the field signals platoons of air-defence artillery units and the parachute troops, the air signals company, once formed and attached to its air formation, remained part of the air signals corps and wore the latter's brown flashes. The company consisted of a headquarters, a headquarters signals platoon serving *Geschwader* headquarters, and platoons which were detached to *Gruppen* but were under command of the *Gruppe* for operational purposes only.

According to the company's war-establishment, the headquarters signals platoon and its detachments were responsible for the establishment and maintenance of communications between the *Geschwader* and higher headquarters, and also for the provision of radio beacon, visual beacon and radio-navigation detachments to the *Gruppen*. But in *KG 51* these navigational aids were always in fact with the signals platoons detached to squadrons and were integrated with them. At least up to 1943, the company remained in fact well overstrength. Thus at times the *Gruppe* signals platoons rose to 120 men and held both a great deal of extra signals equipment that had been allocated to them in the stable period of operations against England and a number of French, British and Russian captured vehicles.

Thanks to this array of equipment, the platoons were able, without outside assistance, to provide squadrons with the complete signals support they needed on a forward airfield. But as a rule, even in wartime, the signals platoons could count on support from existing static branches belonging to the airfield headquarters.

Because of the risk of intercept by the enemy monitoring service, command was exercised as far as possible on telephone and teleprinter links. The signals platoons always provided telephone communications within the *Gruppe*, the number of extensions to headquarters branches and flights depending on the length of stay on one field. Separate systems for dispersal areas and accommodation often proved useful; depending on local conditions, direct lines might be laid or switched through between the ops room and the met office, the navigational aids or local AA units. There were always external links from these switchboards to the airfield exchange, and often direct to *Geschwader* or higher headquarters.

In addition to these telephone links there were the teleprinters. But, especially in mobile operations in the Eastern Front, the teleprinter detachments of the signals company were in the main used simply to reinforce the static teleprinter sections on the airfield.

When these line links were unavailable, destroyed or overloaded, formations went over to ground-to-ground radio. As a general rule a *Geschwader* net was established, but frequently the *Gruppen* became outstations on the nets of headquarters several levels higher.

Short wave W/T was used for ground-air communication. The ground station for this was a heavy short-wave transmitter, the good old Wireless Set GIII or more up-to-date variants of it, known as 'Wireless Set GX', cannibalised from scrap equipment by the men of the signals platoon and mounted on home-made panels. Even Wireless Set GXVI, the air-to-air R/T set of the Ju 88, was built up into an auxiliary ground station by the signallers. To begin with it was used only for listening in to the R/T traffic within a formation; but its range was so good that it was also possible to establish communications from the ground with formations in the air, and this means was used for immediate reports to the ops room of successful engagements and other events.

In *III Gruppe* experiments were also made in the use of the Wireless Set GXVI for forward air control. In summer '42 1st Lieut. Fritsch, the squadron operations officer, an experienced observer, and Lieutenant Boemer, an air radio officer, together with a small signals detachment, were attached to 23 Armoured Division to pass air support requests, front-line situation reports and so on to their squadron in the air, and also under certain circumstances to direct bombing. Unfortunately the *Gruppe* was not committed at the time to operations on the line of contact, so this form of control never came to be used in anger.

The platoons' navigational aids were deployed to improve the static installations on main and forward airfields.

The frequent moves made special demands on the enthusiasm and resourcefulness of the signalmen. Support on the old airfield had to be maintained until the last aircraft had taken off, while at the same time dispersal sites and an operations room had to be established at the new one by the time the *Gruppe* flew in. This was feasible only because the platoons carried well over their scale of signals equipment.

But the key factor was the ability to move the signals advance party with its equipment by air. The drill was to load two of the first flight of Ju 52 transports with radio and line personnel, and this usually proved possible. These two Ju 52 loads sufficed to get the new operations room set up to the point where missions could be flown. The rest of the platoon followed by tedious surface routes—on overcrowded roads which always seemed to be dusty, muddy or iced up—or by rail.

The company commander doubled as *Geschwader* Signals Officer. The *Gruppe* headquarters originally had radio and navigation officers on its own strength, who were responsible for signals and navigational documentation, map supply and briefing of aircrew radio operators. But as the war went on, the only officers trained on airborne radio and the control of instrument flying were signals officers posted into the *Geschwader* signals companies, and *Gruppe* commanders often allotted this task to their signals platoon commander. It was almost unknown for these SOs, as they were generally called, to help out in other functions and to relieve the *Gruppe* operations officer in the operations room.

Since crews which had trained together were usually reluctant to take a strange radio operator on operational missions, few signals officers had a chance to gain much operational experience. Nonetheless they were always pressing to go on operations, and a good number of officers from *KG 51* Motorised Air Signals Company were lost on operations over France, England, the Balkans, the Mediterranean or Russia.

In the course of operations in all theatres the *Geschwader* signals company and the *Gruppe* signals platoons became virtually an integral part of their units. Their unflagging support in establishing and maintaining communications in heat or biting frost, in snow or in mud, round the clock and often in the face of the enemy, earned grateful recognition from commanders, staffs and aircrew, who knew they could always count on their friends of the brown flash.

Extract from Air Force War Establishment No. 3383(L) dated June 1st, 1943.

*1. Summary of Strengths*

| | *Officers* | *NCOs* | *Airmen* | *Vehicles* | *Trailers* | *Motor cycles* |
|---|---|---|---|---|---|---|
| Headquarters Group | 2 | 12 | 14 | 6 | 2 | 1 |
| 1 Platoon, HQ Signals | 1 | 25 | 87 | 25 | – | 3 |
| 2 Platoon Squadron Signals | 1 | 16 | 46 | 14 | 1 | 1 |
| 3 Platoon, Squadron Signals | 1 | 16 | 46 | 14 | 1 | 1 |
| 4 Platoon, Squadron Signals | 1 | 16 | 46 | 14 | 1 | 1 |
| Total excluding medical personnel | 6 | 85 | 239 | 73 | 5 | 7 |

*2. Allocation of Detachments to Platoons*

| | |
|---|---|
| Headquarters Group | 1 Battery Charging Det. (motorised)<br>1 Vehicle Repair Det. |
| 1 Platoon (HQ Signals) (LW) (motorised) | 1 Line Det.<br>2 Teleprint Terminal Dets. (motorised)<br>1 Teleprint Terminal Det.<br>3 Line Construction Dets. (motorised)<br>1 Light Radio Det. (SW/LW) (motorised)<br>2 Light Visual Beacon Dets. (motorised)<br>1 Radio Receiving Det. (motorised)<br>1 Radio Navigation and DF Det. W) (motorised) |
| 2, 3 and 4 Platoons (motorised air signals platoon), *each* | 1 Heavy Radio Det. (SW) (motorised)<br>1 Light Radio Det. (SW) (motorised)<br>1 Line Det. (motorised)<br>1 Light Radio Det. (LW) (motorised)<br>1 Line-Laying Det. (motorised)<br>1 Radio Homing/Blind-Landing Det. |

Appendix F

# *The Bomber Crew*

. . . teamwork in the air, in success and in disaster . . .

The crew of a bomber was made up of: the pilot ('the coachman'), the observer ('Franz'), the radio operator, the air gunner ('Annie') and in some types of aircraft the flight engineer ('the mixer').

In a division of duties based on team spirit the pilot had to fly his aircraft by day and night through icing, fog and cloud, and to control navigation and communications. The observer, whether or not he could see the ground, had to guide the aircraft to the right target and drop the bombs in the right place. The radio operator had to maintain communication not only with the flanking aircraft but also with the various ground stations and navigational systems. The safety of the crew and the feasibility of the mission depended entirely on the flight-engineer/air gunner or on the senior fitter of the ground crew. And on top of all this the whole crew had to be able to shoot straight with the various machine-guns and cannon that might be mounted.

The airman began his service with six-months ground training in a reinforcement training unit. After passing an NCOs' course he was promoted sergeant. Officer cadets and potential officers of the reserve attended an officers' school.

The reinforcement flying schools of the aircrew reinforcement training units looked after preliminary training, aircrew selection and the training of air gunners. Flying in single-engined trainers took place at 'A' and 'B' flying schools, while the 'C' schools carried out continuation training on multi-engined machines up to the stage of instrument flying qualification. The final stages took place in command schools, such as the bomber schools at Fassberg, Jueterborg, Lechfeld, Prenzlau and Tutov. The award of wings or even of the advanced air-force pilot's licence was a prerequisite for the posting of any officer, NCO or airman to a first-line unit as a pilot.

The observer or auxiliary observer briefed the pilot on target approach, kept the navigation plot and log, worked out the heading, acted as bomb-aimer and was responsible for visual and photographic target reconnaissance. Observer training lasted six months.

The radio operator aided the pilot and worked with the observer on navigation; he was also trained and employed as air-gunner. He handled air traffic control, air-to-air and air-to-ground radio traffic, and was responsible for radio navigation and DF. His training took a full year, divided between the air signals and instrument flying schools, and air-gunner training.

The flight engineer was responsible for technical servicing of the aircraft and was also trained in navigation. He was selected from amongst the technical airmen fit for military flying and in principle received air-gunner training.

Crew training began, together with operational conversion and formation training, at the bomber schools and was continued within the unit by a combination of day and night navigational flights in all weathers and intensive bombing and gunnery practice from all heights.

Appendix G

# *About These Bomber Pilots*

by Werner Baumbach

Bomber and fighter pilots were two quite different animals. The nature of the task with its long flights deep into enemy territory, over the sea, in foul weather and at night, its formation attacks and not least the characteristics of the slow-flying bomber itself—all these things put their stamp on the bomber pilot's face, his look of outward calm and dogged persistence—dourness, the fighter pilots used to call it. As the war went on the mastery of his aircraft, especially in the attack itself and in defensive action, made ever-growing demands on the bomber-pilot's versatility.

The fighter pilots came to know our problems from their ground-attack and foul-weather assignments. And so, despite the differences, towards the end of the war there evolved a sort of all-round battle-pilot type. But a good fighter pilot was seldom a good bomber man, and vice-versa. The bomber pilot has always to be on the alert to avoid being shot down. He is constantly on the lookout for aids to survival and evasive measures, but he must not forget what he is there for—to get his bombs to the target. But fighter and bomber men alike, not forgetting the dive-bomber pilots too, were bound by a kind of unspoken, dry comradeship, which encompassed the differences in their make-up and grew stronger as the going got rougher.

Unlike the fighter arm, the bomber force did not present any very coherent image early in the war. Well into 1941, most bomber *Geschwadern* had flown operations which by and large brought few problems of importance with which they were not familiar from training flights. The He 111 and Do 217 usually dropped their bombs in level flight, in formation by day and individually by night. This operating procedure had made it easy for the old staff officers, generals and all, to hold their own and work for their Knight's Crosses. There were of course exceptions, but generally speaking a young lieutenant or captain would assume command of the formation once it was airborne.

It would be right and proper to assert that the bomber force achieved its early successes in the blitzkrieg campaigns with a total absence of leadership at higher formation or even strategic level. At tactical level, it was the young subalterns and captains, the aircraft captains and *Staffel* leaders, who set the pace. Their mentality, their style of life, their bearing and manner, the exuberance of their talk and the dash which carried their men with them contrasted so glaringly with the clipped accents, heel-clicking, parade-ground manner and dependence on outward appearances of the veterans, fetched down off the shelf and dusted off, that, as the war went on, an unbridgeable crevasse split the bomber force into two camps. The staff-majors were on the side of youth; these were war veterans whose idealism had kept them true to flying in civilian life and so kept their hearts young. Where should we have been without them—these reserve officers who rejoined the first-line formations as maids of all work?

Technology too played its part in deepening the rift between the two generations. In the Ju 88 the pilot was the captain; he gave the orders for the tactics as well as the flight procedures; in dive-bombing he himself released his bombs. The observer's role was limited to bomb-aiming in horizontal flight and to help with navigation. This asked a very great deal of the pilot/captain; but it served to put us in the same position as the fighter pilot. And the Ju 88 had too little room in it to take an extra crew member as ballast, as could be done in the He 111 and Do 217. It looked as if the aged formation commander's hour had struck.

Further, from among the young officers who had graduated at Staff College just before the war, some of those posted to first-line units were the ideal type of air commander. Sadly there were too few of them—and many of them had all too little time to live. But they included, to name just two, the commander of the first Ju 88 *Geschwader* Lieutenant Colonel Loebel, and his *Gruppe* leader, Major Doerich. They used their brains and led by example. A new style of discipline and a firm unsentimental comradeship spurred this *Geschwader* on to outstanding success and soon made it the spiritual home of the first-rate professional bomber crew.

As 1941 went by, other *Geschwadern* were converted to Ju 88s. But in some of these the 'old men' fought a strong rearguard action. Their main prop was an old fossil of a general, of the highest personal qualities but much given to formality, who as Head of Personnel was about as much good to the young Air Force as Methuselah would have been to Cleopatra. Rejuvenation potions wouldn't bring us any laurels from that quarter! So on the spur of the moment I decided to go to the Chief of Air Staff, who for all his forty years was young in heart and on the side of youth; and he passed my representation on to Goering.

The direct result of this intervention, which coincided with a report along the same lines from Captain Peltz, was that by the end of 1941 a school for bomber formation commanders had been set up and Peltz, one of the most talented young bomber pilots, had been put in command of it.

Goering gave Peltz unheard-of freedom of action. From then on, no one could be appointed to command of a first-line formation unless he had passed out at this school. The 'old men' too had to go there for a check-up, and this quickly sorted the sheep from the goats. These courses quickly became the focus of a young group of commanders, but also of vigorous opposition to everything behind the first line, opposition to the Air Staff, the higher headquarters, the Ministry of Aviation and the Party big-wigs alike. But these men remained loyal to the Fuehrer and to their Commander-in-Chief, Goering, who did everything for his airmen when the going was good and who, as a man, often showed an infectious comradeliness, concern and generosity; he could have found his strongest support in this circle of young 'sharp end' officers when things began to go wrong.

This rejuvenation treatment of the operational fighter pilots and bomber crews was accompanied by a reorganisation of the inspectorates of fighters and bombers. After Moelders' fatal crash, Galland became Directot of Fighters; and at the end of 1942 I was posted from the Mediterranean to Berlin and, jointly with Peltz, appointed Director of Bambers. Our responsibilities now extended to training, the tactical and technical evaluation of battle experience, operational requirements and selections for command appointments. On top of this we were given a certain power of veto vis-a-vis the Air Staff with the Commander-in-Chief of the *Luftwaffe*.

But the deep divisions between first-line units and higher command could not be resolved. They went about fighting the war so differently that only the highest personal and professional qualities could build a lasting bridge. This meant that, as the war dragged on, the areas of operations expanded and enemy superiority mounted, the demands made on first-line formations became more and more exacting. Only by superior leadership and team-work between crews could an operation succeed. In bomber flying, star rating went more and more out of fashion. In a night attack or in foul weather, who even wanted to know which crew's bombs had scored the best hits? The achievement of the formation as a whole was what mattered; and success turned on skilful and determined leadership.

Thus the concepts and notions of the First World War had run full circle. Then, for instance, it was the fighter which was king of the air, now it was the bomber. Admittedly this about-face to some extent stemmed from technical redefinition; nevertheless it was not entirely without significance. In fact it characterised the shift in the focal point of air warfare. In 1914–18 the fighter pilot bore the brunt of the air war and was thus regarded as king of the air; but now he had to cede his role and the title that goes with it to the bomber man. In simple terms, the bomber force should be the backbone of air warfare. Influenced as it was by the theories of Dounet and Rougeron, this was the ruling view of the German High Command both during the build-up of the *Luftwaffe* and in the war. This was the basis on which designers and technologists had created the German bomber; and they believed their aircraft to be almost invulnerable and unassailable—indeed superior to all foreign fighters. Right at the beginning of the war the first-line units learnt the hard way how wrong this view was. Nevertheless, the High Command and the great majority of engineers in official posts stuck to their guns and continued to think that they could win the war with these once so successful bombers.

Appendix H

# *Flight Procedures for 'Silver' – the Me 262*

I *Starting*

1 Inboard generator switches, left and right; press control for starter ignition and metering systems. (*Warning*. The arrangement of these controls is not the same in all aircraft.)

2 Start run-up motor, and after 3–5 seconds clutch in; switch rev. counter to low range, at 800 rpm press ignition button. At 2,000 rpm declutch run-up motor, move throttle *slowly* forward keeping ignition button pressed, open fuel-cock, switch on fuel delivery pumps, lock idling limiters. At 3000 rpm release ignition button.

3 Switch on tank pumps.

*II* *After Starting*

1 Switch remote control switches to 'on'. Switch on automatic switches for artificial horizon, trimmer and (if required) pilot head heater.

2 Switch on Type 16 radio.

3 For airfield R/T, select Channel 3.

4 Uncage artificial horizon.

*III* *Running Up*

1 Check chocks in position.

2 Run up each engine separately.

3 Move throttle *slowly* forward up to 6,000rpm (watch temperature), then in a single firm movement to full throttle.

4 At 8,100rpm check see sheet. (Check on differential gas pressure and visual check on exhaust cone.)

5 Differential gas pressure should be 10–12psi

6 Fuel pressure 850psi, oil pressure 15–60psi, temperature not above red mark.

7 Move throttle back in a single firm movement.

*IV Taxing*

1 Shut canopy hood properly. (*Warning*. Make sure lever is locked in closed position.)
2 Move throttles *slowly* forward, watching that temperature does not go above the red mark.
3 Taxi slowly straight ahead.
4 Steer on the brakes. (Make sure you don't taxi too slowly or there may be problems with the nose-wheel.)
5 Brakes must operate faultlessly (otherwise aircraft unserviceable).

*V. Preparation for Take-Off*

1 Line up aircraft for take-off.
2 Apply both brakes.
3 Trim setting up to 3° nose-down, depending on fuel load.
4 Flaps at 20°.
5 Check communications with ground control.

*VI Take-Off*

1 Press stopwatch.
2 Open throttles to 7,000rpm
3 Release brakes and open throttles fully.
4 Check readings for both engines.
5 Control column in normal position. The aircraft should move straight ahead; correct any deviation on the brakes.
6 At 110–125mph, lift off. Do not pull too hard on the control colum (this will produce an excessive angle of incidence), and make a brief correcting movement.
7 Brake wheels.
8 Push lock to left and press 'undercarriage retract' button. The button will spring out when the undercarriage is fully retracted. (Try to avoid exceeding 160mph during retraction.)
9 Cruising revs 8,000–8,300rpm; 8,000 for circuits.
10 Flaps up before speed reaches 225mph.
11 Trim aircraft to normal attitude.

*VII In Flight*

1 Watch engine instruments.
2 Watch fuel supply.
3 Monitor automatic switch buttons.

*VIII Preparation for Landing*

1 Throttle back to 6,500rpm

2 Pull control column back to reduce speed (to 200–225mph).
3 Press 'undercarriage down' button. (*Warning*. As the undercarriage is lowered, the aircraft will suddenly become tail-heavy.) Correct speed to 185mph
4 Indicator lights for undercarriage and nosewheel *must* light up ('Down'), as this is the only check.
5 Flaps to 20°.
6 With undercarriage down, maintain speed above 175mph during turns.
7 Correct control column pressures by trimming.

*IX Landing*

1 Adopt normal glide angle.
2 Flaps fully out. Hold 160mph, reducing to 145–140mph on approach.
3 At end of runway put the aircraft down (Landing speed 125–115mph).
4 Pull throttle back to idling position. (*Warning*. Do not pull right back to 'Stop' or flame-back will occur.)
5 Pull the control column back in the usual way up to touchdown. Keep the nosewheel off the ground and then let down slowly onto it.
6 Taxi to rest, braking if necessary. Flaps in.

*X Special Procedures*

1 *Engine Cut Out*. Close fuel-cock, throttle to 'Stop', delivery pump off, correct on rudder.
2 *Flying on One Engine* is entirely feasible. Turns over both running and windmilling engines are feasible. The aircraft will climb.
3 *Landing on One Engine* is entirely feasible. (*Warning*. If the port engine is shut down, operate undercarriage and flaps by compressed air.) Landing procedure normal. Speed on approach circuit not below 165mph.
4 *Overshoot*. Open throttles slowly. Retract undercarriage at or above 190mph. Bring flaps in gradually.
5 *Baling Out*. If possible reduce speed to 220mph. Unplug helmet connections. Jettison hood. Free harness. (The method of leaving the aircraft is left to the individual pilot's initiative.)

# *Bibliography*

As the subtitle of this history of *Kampfgeschwader 51* (Edelweiss) indicates, the author has attempted to put together a chronicle based on documents and reports, and statements by former members of the unit. Being of the post-war generation and having therefore no battle experience, he had of course no choice but to evaluate and digest a mass of complementary documentation. In addition to papers belonging to former members of Edelweiss *Geschwader* many of whom proved to be most active and helpful collaborators, background material was drawn from the following publications.

Kriegstagebuch III./Kampfgeschwader 51 (Abschrift)
Karl Bartz 'Als der Himmel brannte' Hannover 1955
Werner Baumbach 'Zu spät?' München 1949
Cajus Bekker 'Angriffshöhe 4000' Oldenburg 1964
Wulf Bley 'Deutschland zur Luft' Stuttgart 1939
Paul Carell 'Unternehmen Barbarossa' Berlin 1963
'Verbrannte Erde', dto. 1966
Hellmuth Günther Dahms 'Der zweite Weltkrieg', BMVg 1966
J. Diakow 'Generaloberst Alexander Löhr' Freiburg 1964
Georg W. Feuchter 'Geschichte des Luftkrieges' Bonn 1954
Adolf Galland 'Die Ersten und die Letzten' Darmstadt 1953
Galland-Ries-Ahnert 'Die Deutsche Luftwaffe 1939–1945' Bad Nauheim ohne Jahrgang
Hans-Adolf Jacobsen 'Der zweite Weltkrieg in Chronik und Dokumenten' Darmstadt 1959
Kens-Nowarra 'Die deutschen Flugzeuge 1933–1945' München 1961
Ploetz 'Geschichte des Zweiten Weltkrieges' Würzburg 1960

Josef Priller 'Geschichte eines Jagdgeschwaders' Heidelberg 1962
Karl Ries jr. 'Markierungen und Tarnanstriche der Luftwaffe im Zweiten Weltkrieg' Band 1–4, Mainz 1963
'Dora Kurfürst und die rote 13', Band 1–4, dto. 1966
Hans-Detlef Herhudt von Rohden 'Die Luftwaffe ringt um Stalingrad' Wiesbaden 1950
Gerhard von Seemen 'Die Ritterkreuzträger 1939–1945' Bad Nauheim 1955
Karl-Heinz Völker 'Die Deutsche Luftwaffe 1933–1939' Stuttgart 1967
Dr Theo Weber 'Die Luftschlacht um England' CH Frauenfeld 1956

# *Acknowledgements*

The author wishes to record his special gratitude for the cooperation, suggestions and support of: the German Red Cross (Missing Persons Department); the German War Graves Commission; the German Office for Notification of Next of Kin of Members of the former Wehrmacht killed on active service (WAST); the Central Information Office of the Federal Archives; Specialist Panel VI (Air Forces and History of Air Warfare) of the Bureau for Military Historical Research; and the following individual collaborators:

Rudolf Abrahamczik
Egon Arz
Wolfgang Baetz
Siegfried Barth
Prof Dr Ing Wilhelm Batel
Helmut Bernhardt
Hans Heinrich Bömer
Buck
Christian Burkhardt
Alfred Delles
Fritzherbert Dierich
Fridl Fath
Karl-Heinz Feldmann
Heinz Fietze
Alfred Fritsch
Dr Karl Gundelach

Dr Hans Gutzmer
Klaus Häberlen
Hanns Heise
Ernst Hinrichs
Hans Hoiss
Hans Holzwarth
Theo Jäger
Reinhold Joos
Josef Kammhuber
Ludwig Kliebenstein
Dr Hermann Kölbel
Heinrich Kratzert
Helmut Kroll
Walter Lau
Siegfried Lauterwasser
Ronny Lauer
Günther Löffelbein
Fritz Lutz
Alfred Mahncke
Albert Maser
Wolf Meister
Herbert Meyer
Albert Mittelmann
Hans Moser
Ernst Obermaier
Cornelie Pfeiffer
Ernst Pflüger
Ludwig Piller
Joachim Poetter
Horst Puls
Dr Else Rath
Bernd Sartor
Friedrich Scheel
Lothar Schilling
Josef Schölss
Adolf Schwachenwald
Gerda Schwiegk/Scholz
Heinrich Schwipp
Wolfgang Seils
Dr Karl-Heinz Stahl
Klaus Thoms
Heinz Unrau
Dr Rolf Woernle
Georg Zepf
Uwe Zimmermann
Hans-Joachim Zogel

VITEBSK
SMOLENSK
VILNA
ROSLAVL
MINSK
BOBRUISK
GOMEL
R. DESNA
POLAND
WARSAW
BREST-LITOFSK
LUBLIN
VLADIMIR
LUTSK
KIEV
SCHITOMIR
BERDITCHEV
R. VISTULA
LEMBERG
TARNOPOL
CRACOW
R. DNIESTER
R. BUG
CZERNOWITZ
BALTA
BALTI
TIRASPOL
ODESSA
HUNGARY
KLAUSENBURG
ROMANIA
ZILISTEA
BELGRADE
BUCHAREST
R. DANUBE
YUGOSLAVIA
SOFIA
BULGARIA
PLOVDIV
ISTANBUL
SALONIKA
KORCA